GANESHA
goes to LUNCH

Classics from Mystic India

MANDALA
PUBLISHING

San Rafael, Calif.

GANESHA
goes to LUNCH
Classics from Mystic India

Kamla K. Kapur

MANDALA
PUBLISHING

MANDALA
PUBLISHING

Mandala Publishing
10 Paul Drive
San Rafael, CA 94903
www.mandalapublishing.com
800.688.2218

www.kamlakkapur.com

Three of these stories were originally published in *Parabola* magazine.
They are: "The Snake Who Lost His Hiss" Volume 24, No.4 (Issue on Evil)
"The Bird Who Fought War" Volume 27, No. 4 (Issue on War)
"Indra Gets Caught" Volume 28, No. 4 (Issue on Truth and Illusion)

Library of Congress Cataloging-in-Publication Data available.

ISBN: 978-1-60109-102-4

 ♻ REPLANTED PAPER

ROOTS of PEACE

Insight Editions, in association with Roots of Peace, will plant two trees for each tree
used in the manufacturing of this book. Roots of Peace is an internationally renowned
humanitarian organization dedicated to eradicating land mines worldwide and converting
war-torn lands into productive farms and wildlife habitats. Together, we will plant two
million fruit and nut trees in Afghanistan and provide farmers there with the skills and
support necessary for sustainable land use.

Manufactured in China by Insight Editions.

10 9 8 7 6 5 4

Cover image © Charan Sharma
The illustrations included in thes book are by the great modern Indian masters B.G.
Sharma and Indra Sharma. Their artwork is explored in more detail and reproduced in
full color in these titles from Mandala Publishing:

Form of Beauty: The Krishna Art of B.G. Sharma
with text by Swami B.V. Tripurari

In a World of Gods and Goddesses: The Mystic Art of Indra Sharma
with text by James H. Bae

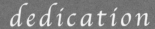

dedication

to
My father, Brigadier Hardit Singh Kapur,
My mother, Lajwant Kaur
Who told me many enlightening stories

and to
My husband, Payson R. Stevens,
Without whom this book
Would never have been

TABLE OF CONTENTS

Author's Preface...8

STORIES OF VISHNU...12

Introduction...13
On the Track of Love...14
Entirely Entangled...24
Vishnu Forgets...33
Out of Vishnu's Mouth...38

STORIES OF BRAHMA...44

Introduction...45
How Brahma Created the Dream...46
Indra Gets Caught...51

STORIES OF SHIVA, PARVATI, AND GANESHA...54

Introduction...55
The Marriage of Shiva and Parvati...56
How Ganesha got his Elephant Head...62
Ganesha goes to Lunch...71

A STORY OF KRISHNA AND SOME PARABLES...78

Introduction...79
The Million Steps ...80
The Snake Who Lost His Hiss...88
Hermits...90
From the Eyes of Stars...92

STORIES FROM THE RAMAYANA...94

Introduction...95
The Sinews of his Spirit ...96
Ashes and Dust ...101
The Toad who didn't Croak...107
Hanuman Bares All ... 111
The Lowly, Holy Staff...115

STORIES FROM THE MAHABHARATA...122

Introduction...123
The Deer People ...124
See Him in the Dark ...130
You...138
The Bird Who Fought War ...143
Blind Hunger ...147
Elsewhere Bound ...150

AUTHOR'S PREFACE

For half the year, every year, my husband and I live in a remote valley in the Kullu district of the Himalayas in India. The region is called devbhumi, "the earth of the gods," or more commonly, "Valley of the Gods." India's mythic past is present here, pulsing and alive in the names of trees, rivers, villages, and temples.

Ubiquitous in this thousand-year old forest is the *Cedrus deodara*, cedar, or deodar, divine wood, tree of the gods. The stream that flows in front of our house is named "Hirub," after Hidamba, one of Bheem's wives, sister of a demon that he slew. Bheem is one of five Pandava brothers, the heroes of the great Indian epic, the *Mahabharata*.

The temple in the village after which the stream is named, and which is an hour of vigorous hiking away from our home, has a temple dedicated to Panch Vir, the five heroes of the epic. The temple in our own little village is dedicated to Boodhi Nagan, Old Serpent Woman, who is said to have hosted the five brothers in their exile. Vishnu Narayana, Shiva, and Kali also have their temples in the area. At least three or four times a week, loud horns and drums announce a peregrinating god or goddess on his or her visit to other temples or villages to attend a marriage or bless a new birth, a new house, a wedding, or a retirement. The particular god or goddess is represented by a brass mask under a canopy of silver, atop a palanquin decorated with brightly colored scarves of silk and satin, bordered with gold, and adorned with brilliant local flowers.

What is found in this valley is an intensified reflection of that mythic connection that is strong even in urban India. The majority of the Hindu population is actively engaged with mythic practice. It is not uncommon to see naked, ash-smeared sadhus, disciples of Lord Shiva, walking barefoot on the roads, a python around their necks, or even riding motorcycles, matted locks flying. Even the more staid believers worship gods from mythology. The names of God are the same as the names of characters from the epics: Krishna, Shiva, Vishnu, and Rama. Men, and women too, are named after these gods. Many national holidays are dedicated to Shiva, Ganesha, and Krishna. Even large corporations carry ads in the papers: "Happy Birthday, Krishna!" Pictures and statues of Ganesha are found on websites, wedding cards, invitations to and announcements of marriages, births, and birthdays. Plastic, stone, and clay images of these gods adorn dashboards of cars, entrances to shops, restaurants, homes and offices. In the countryside too, in fields and forests, under trees, over roofs, in caves, and by roadsides, statues of gods have their dwellings.

India has a vast and inexhaustible storehouse of mythic stories. I say "inexhaustible" because there are manifold versions of each myth. The oral beginnings of mythology ensured that there were very few authorized and definitive "originals." Over the centuries there have been additions, interpolations, revisions, and accretions that have swelled the streams of stories to rivers and oceans. Then again, each of the many regions and languages of India has adapted the myths to its ethos, with the result that the same myth is so substantially different from one version to another as to constitute an entirely new story. India's tradition of anonymous creativity has further added to the storehouse without leaving any trace of authorship.

Even today, holy men continue to take strands from the epics and spin parables from them to instruct and illuminate their congregations: undoubtedly the story of the toad from the Ramayana, herein retold, or the two stories, "Blind Hunger" and "The Bird Who Fought War," from the Mahabharata, told to me verbally and of which I have found no mention in my extensive research, fall in this category. It would not be too far-fetched to say that Indian mythology is a work in progress, still being evolved. It is this undiscovered treasure-trove of written texts and oral tradition that makes the study of Indian myth bewildering and rewarding.

More than in any other culture I know, myth is alive and well in India. What is in-your-face here is a reminder of the hidden truth that myth has informed all the cultures of the world; that it is, in fact, the root of all religion, spirituality, and art. The mythology of the world—as Joseph Campbell, the great popularizer of myth in the twentieth century, has taught us—is essentially one shape-shifting story. The global village is deeply linked, as our etymologies and a great deal of other evidence manifest. One has but to look at the root of, say, the word deodar, to see the invisible meta-reality that links us all, like the subterranean, entwined roots of a dense forest: Germanic, Old English, Old Norse, Sanskrit, Latin, and Avestan myths and words are inextricably interconnected.

To use another metaphor, the mythology of the world is one gem whose manifold facets are created and polished by different cultures. The myths of every culture illumine aspects of the same essential mystery. Western mythology, as the works of Jung, Freud, and countless others have revealed, illumine the dark recesses of the mind, and offer deep, psychological insights into the human psyche. The aspect that Indian myth brings to the surface of consciousness is, predictably, the spiritual and philosophic.

All mythic stories that are not mere fanciful and primitive explanations of natural phenomenon exist at the interface between form and the formless, matter and energy. As a vessel is necessary to contain shapeless water; as a book, words; as sound, meaning; images, or "masks," as Campbell calls them, concretize the abstract mystery of life. While all myth—or for that matter, all art—gives form and substance to that one, formless energy that manifests as life within and around us, Indian myth in particular has "a genius for clothing the infinite in human form," as Eknath Easwaran puts it in his book, *The Thousand Names of Vishnu*. The function of many Indian myths is to take us through duration, through the conflict and turmoil of the secular, melodramatic, human story, to the timeless, eternal beyond, the faceless and imageless source, the beginnings and endings of our terrestrial journey.

It is easy to see how Indian myth has become the repository of all our wisdom and solace. The gods, like us, are all perishable, yet timeless, like Vishnu asleep on the primeval ocean, appearing and disappearing in his incarnations like bubbles in the river of time. There is in the threads of these narratives a deep and unshakeable conviction of the deathlessness of all that is. The animate and inanimate world is formed out of the same indestructible energy. The myths seem to say to the doubting, earth-bound self, that the plasma that created all of us is, as we move through our often tragic and joyful journey, permeable to prayer. For how can a universe that has created in humans their most intense longing for the divine within and around them, thwart it? It is this assurance, so plainly and convincingly demonstrated in the stories, that makes them the hypostasis of this culture, and invites the fascination of others, the West in particular.

As India becomes a major player of the twenty-first century and comes into economic ascendancy, the West would do well to remember that India's gift to humankind is not just its emergent information and pharmaceutical technologies. There is something far more valuable that India has to offer the world.

For those of us compelled to make the journey of life a conscious endeavor, the central question how to live cannot be answered without first addressing the question, how to think. Enough research in psychology, philosophy, and physics has been done in the twentieth century to confirm that the imagination—not facts, not wealth or an accumulation of material goods, not name brands, or high paying jobs—constitutes the substance of "reality." Not our eyes alone, but the consciousness behind them that sees, determines the quality of our experience of life.

Indian philosophy and mythology—the latter being the concrete expression of the former abstraction—makes it its business to investigate this consciousness.

The twenty-four stories herein retold and developed from India's rich and vast ocean of Hindu myths, legends, and folktales are a mix of well-known classics with a modern twist, and stories told to me verbally. Their timeless quality lends itself to reinterpretation in every age. Many of these tales came to me as fragments—a few sentences, a paragraph at the most. Where I found the bare bones of a plot, I restructured it. Development of the narrative has been my primary focus. I have at all times tried to retain the essence rather than stick to the particular circumstance, or version of a myth. The manifold aspects of these gems allowed me to uncover and polish yet another facet of their relevance and brilliance.

I have been a lover of Indian mythology, having heard and read many stories in my childhood and youth from my parents, my teachers, movies, and comic books. It was not until I went to the United States for graduate studies that myth became a conscious discipline. I studied it, taught it, and formulated it. Yet these stories have not evolved out of any systematic study of Indian mythology. I selected them by a process that I call "instinctive preference." I picked the story that made me stop in my tracks, that engendered a "spark" that I recognized instinctively as a symptom of profound interest on my part.

And as I worked on the stories, they revealed their essence, modern pertinence, and the reason why my heart had preferred them to countless others. These narratives of the soul's journey from ignorance to light instructed me, illumined my path, transported me to a transcendent space of mystery and magic, and set me wondering at the human condition.

Life is infinitely more marvelous than our day-to-day business and work, money and illness, family and bosses would make it seem. It is precisely the function of myth to thrust us out of the quotidian into the miraculous. One lives life more deeply, with greater peace and joy, when one lives with the enigmas that permeate it. These stories warp our minds, and allow us a perspective on life, on its incredible, enmeshing, magic web of Maya, and the dreamlike nature of our experience on this planet. These myths are reminders from spaceless eternity of the stuff of which our bodies, minds, souls, and spirits are made. They wake us up, and help us live with, and within, the mystery that is the matrix of our being.

STORIES OF
VISHNU

Introduction to the Stories of Vishnu

*V*ishnu, the Preserver, is the central god in four of the stories that follow. He is one of the three main gods of Hindu mythology, along with Brahma, Creator of the World, and Shiva, the Destroyer. There is, however, a lot of healthy contradiction in, and a great deal of overlapping of, their roles.

Brahma, the Creator, for example, is born out of the navel of Vishnu, the Preserver. The Hindu view of the world sees both creation and destruction as a dance within an underlying force, which endures beneath the flux of being and not being, life and death, and all the other contraries of life.

The root of Vishnu's name, vish, means "to pervade," hence Vishnu means "he who is everywhere and at all times." Traditional iconography depicts Vishnu as sleeping blissfully on the coiled body of Shesh Nag, a serpent who floats upon the primeval ocean. Shesh Nag's fanned hoods form the canopy of Vishnu's bed. Vishnu can also be seen flying on his mount or vehicle, the great swan—or Parmahansa—named Garuda. The world is Vishnu's dream. Vishnu, with all his complexity, has a thousand names. One of them is Narayana, from Nara, or "waters," and means "the Prime Being who sleeps upon the waters." The name Narayana also stands for "the One, supreme God, Lord of the Universe," and refers to all three gods. Even though Vishnu's bliss lies in sleeping and dreaming the world, he incarnated ten different times—as a human and several animals—to rescue earth from evil and destruction.

Krishna, one of Vishnu's incarnations, and his main love, Radha, make cameo appearances in this section as well. I say his "main" love because Krishna is the Beloved and the Lover of all. He plays his flute and lures the listeners who, forgetting business, duty, and chore, leave their comfortable and secure homes to seek him out in the forest where the god dances, enraptured and enrapturing. Krishna appears again in some of the stories from the epic Mahabharata that conclude this book.

Shiva, Lord of Destruction, is the most contrary god of all. He will be introduced later at length. In this section he appears briefly as Vishnu's nemesis. Shiva is the god of control, who can't tolerate ungodly behavior on the part of other deities who partake of human folly. This, of course, is only part of his character. Contradictions abound.

Narada is an immortal, heavenly musician who plays the vina, the Indian lute. A great devotee of Vishnu, Narada accompanies him on many of his journeys through space-time. And because contrariness is inherent in most of the characters in Hindu mythology, Narada is often also known as a troublemaker.

The thing to remember about all three gods—Brahma, Vishnu, and Shiva—is that they are at once divine characters in the story of life, and also the Over Soul, or Supreme Energy of the world—self-existent, timeless, immeasurable, absolute, unborn, unbounded, uncreated, and deathless.

ON THE TRACK OF LOVE

S itting by the ocean in a garden beneath the blooming horse chestnut tree, the sun shining, and the birds singing, Narada plucked
the strings of his lute and listened to the sound vibrating in concentric
circles around him. "Namo, I bow to Vishnu!" he began. Then again,
"Vishnu, Namo! Namo! Namo!"

He hummed the melody he was composing, and more words and
images came to him as he looked about and saw bees humming around
him, crawling into the clustered horse chestnut flowers rising above
their leaves like lighted candles. He thumped the body of his lute with
one hand to work out the rhythm, his body swaying and jerking to the
beat of the song. It took just the briefest moment to put together the
words, the melody, the beat, after which it all happened simultane-
ously, the song pouring out of him, a little haltingly at first, and then
smoothly, like a river of music.

Narada was overwhelmed by the beauty of the song and awed at his
own composition. Who could rival him in his devotion to Vishnu? His
entire life revolved around Vishnu, singing his praises, talking to him
and about him, loving him, quarreling with him. Narada chuckled to
himself. It is important to quarrel with your god sometimes because it
clears the air and gets you back on the track of love. And in fact, Vishnu
didn't mind. No, on the contrary, he loved Narada in return. How
could he not? Who could sing his praises the way Narada could? Narada
admired himself for admiring Vishnu, and then shutting his eyes, he
sang the marvelous song all over again, fluidly, with passion. He knew

that whenever he sang thus, Vishnu always appeared, and Narada wanted him to appear now and listen to his latest, and best, composition.

And sure enough, when Narada had finished his devotional song, he opened his eyes, and there sat Vishnu, one leg on the other knee, leaning forward, and smiling at Narada with an enigmatic smile.

"Narada," said Vishnu, "how would you like to make a trip to the south of India?"

"Why? What should I do there? You are everywhere. No, I don't want to go anywhere. I just want to sit here in this garden and compose another song to you. Wasn't this last one glorious? Shall I sing it again?"

"Not now, Narada. Go to the tip of India and pay a visit to Muthu Mohan. He is a great devotee of mine."

"Vishnu, you have devotees everywhere, but I'm your favorite. You know I am. Nobody can be better than me."

"No, Narada, Muthu Mohan is a greater devotee than you."

Narada's heart sank and jealousy gripped his heart. "Why, does he compose songs to you?"

"No, he doesn't sing at all."

Narada felt better all of a sudden.

"He has neither a fine voice, nor the talent, nor time. Go meet him, then come back and sing to me, and I shall return," Vishnu said, and disappeared.

"He's just teasing me," Narada thought. "I don't for an instant believe this Muthu Mohan is a greater devotee than me, but I'll go in any case to see what this 'great devotee of mine' is all about."

The day was so beautiful that Narada decided to set out on foot, to feast on the sights of the earth. A little further along, when he grew weary, he pushed off with his toes into the air, and flew leisurely, watching the clouds passing him in both directions.

"My love for Vishnu helps me to levitate and fly," Narada thought. "I'm sure this 'great devotee of mine,' Muthu Mohan, can't do that. And how, anyway, could a devotee pray better in prose than in song? Oh, Vishnu, Vishnu, I know you are just sending me off on a fool's errand, and I'm doing it for love of you. All for the love of you."

And here Narada began improvising another song that began, "all for the love of you . . . you . . . you." Aloft in the clouds, freed of gravity, he curled himself into different positions and played his lute. He put it behind his back and played it there. He could even play with his toes. And his nose. What a catchy tune it was! How it would make everyone dance!

From the corner of his eye Narada saw how even the white clouds stood still to listen to him. Looking down, he saw a parched and desolate desert. Narada began to play a rain melody, and as he did, the clouds grew dark and dense with moisture, and before long began to rain down in torrents. "Can Muthu Mohan do this?" Narada laughed, watching with delight the deluge in the desert.

Confident that there was nothing to worry about at all, Narada quickened his flight, soaring over rivers and the lush coastal areas of South India to where the three great seas meet and merge their waters before a temple to the Virgin Princess, Kanya Kumari. It was evening, and the village was dark. High in the sky Narada couldn't resist playing around some more to announce his arrival. He sang a melody of light, and all the candles and lamps lit themselves, their flames dancing in the night.

Narada landed in Muthu Mohan's backyard. He wasn't going to give away his presence just yet. He wanted to spy on this "great devotee" to see what was so special about him.

As it happened, Muthu Mohan was just washing up the pots and pans after dinner, rubbing his brass utensils with ash from his hearth, and polishing them to a shine. A little girl of about four or five was pouring water from a bucket over the spoons and ladles, and trying to rinse them with her little hands. When the dishes were done, Muthu Mohan took out the banana leaves they had used as plates, and fed them to the neighbor's cows. Then he swept the floor while the child snuggled into her bed, falling asleep soon thereafter. Muthu Mohan turned towards a little alcove in the corner of his hut, which held a statue of Vishnu, some flowers, and a clay incense holder. He lit some sandalwood incense, folded his hands, prayed, and then went over to his bed, lay down, and slept.

"Two minutes!" thought Narada. "See that?" Narada addressed himself to Vishnu in his mind. "Two minutes is all he gave you! This 'great devotee!'"

Narada was assured Vishnu was terribly mistaken. Narada devoted all his days to him! "But, let me spy some more!" he thought.

Narada entered Muthu Mohan's dreams to see if perhaps something was going on there that he didn't know anything about. But no, the man's dreams were not about Vishnu but about haggling over the price of vegetables and a fight with his boss about not getting overtime pay, which ended in Muthu Mohan being fired. So disturbed was Muthu Mohan by this dream that he awoke in a panic. But then, saying "Vishnu! Vishnu," he soon fell back into a deep and dreamless sleep.

The next morning Narada was awakened too early for his liking by the sounds of loud gargling. Muthu Mohan was doing his ablutions, scrubbing his armpits as he bathed. Then he cooked a rice porridge for his daughter, made some tea, packed lunches in banana leaves for himself and his child, cleaned up, readied her for school, hauled a sack of rice on his back, dropped off his girl at school on the way, and walked two miles to the neighboring city, sold his sack of rice, then finally went off to a kiln to bake bricks.

During that day, Narada visited Muthu Mohan's head several times, but discovered no thoughts of Vishnu, just the usual clutter of quotidian chores and worries, and a lot of presence of mind as Muthu Mohan baked the bricks with care, ate his meager lunch, worked some more, then walked back home to the village, carrying construction materials to sell there.

Back at home Muthu Mohan greeted his child who had been picked up from school by a neighbor, and repeated the activities of the evening before. But this time when Muthu Moran prayed, Narada decided to spy on his prayer. He had seen nothing so far that distinguished this Muthu Mohan. But perhaps the secret lay in how he prayed?

Muthu Mohan folded his hands, cleared his mind of all the day's pre-occupations, created a space that was empty, focused in on Vishnu with a single mind, opened his heart wide, and invited Vishnu into it. And there was Vishnu, suddenly present in all his sweetness, laying his hand on Muthu Mohan's head in a blessing, embracing him with his light.

"Oh!" cried Narada, seething with jealousy. So upset was he that Vishnu could enter anybody's heart but his own, that he quickly exited Muthu Mohan's consciousness, and writhed with anger. His agitation was so immense that he simply couldn't settle down. He didn't want to call on Vishnu, at whom he was furious, to help calm him down. So he rushed off into Muthu Mohan's backyard and sat there, pulling at the tuft of hair that hung like a ponytail behind his head. But, though he tried to lock Vishnu out of his heart, a memory floated into his consciousness.

In his incarnation as Krishna, Vishnu had invited Radha, his special and dearest love, to come and dance with him in the dead of night in the forest of Vrindavana by the banks of the river Jamuna. Narada was there, too—for wherever Vishnu was, in whichever reincarnation, dur-

ing whichever epoch in the gyrations of time, Narada accompanied him as his shadow.

It was Raas Lila, the night all the village women dressed up and stepped out of their homes, lured by the sound of Krishna's flute. Radha was dressed in all her finery, for it was she that Krishna was to dance with in the center of the circle formed by his other admir-ers. And he, Narada, had transported himself into Radha's body and Radha's heart, so that he, too, could dance with his Lord, love him the way a woman

loves her beloved and merges with him. Oh, how intense and passionate the experience was! Radha had closed her eyes and Narada had tasted the exquisite taste of loving with his eyes shut. Only briefly did Radha open them to look at her beloved, but oh, the shock of it, the pain, the terror of illusions shattered! For there was Krishna, not only in her arms, but in the arms of every woman dancing there!

Radha had broken away from Krishna's embrace, and run away into the thicket, sobbing her heart out. And Krishna had followed her, and endeavored for what seemed like a thousand years to woo her back, explaining again and again how he had the ability to multiply himself into as many Krishnas as there were devotees—not just mere copies or reflections or fragments of himself—but all of himself, everywhere at once.

In his deep, sonorous, hypnotic voice, Krishna recited to Radha:

om poornamadah poornamidam poornaat poornamudachyate
poornasya poornamaadaaya poornamevaavasishyate

Krishna explained how the whole remains whole, even when something is taken out of it; that what is taken out of the whole is also whole. And that when the whole is taken out of the whole, the whole still remains whole.

But Radha couldn't even conceive of the idea. How could this be? It was untrue! And terribly false of Krishna to make her believe in something that absolutely couldn't be. After hours and hours of this, Krishna had touched his finger to her forehead, removed the curtain of illusion, and Radha's brain had unfurled in unimaginable ways so she could perceive for her own self how Krishna, all of him, in all his entirety, could inhabit every atom in the universe!

Radha had come away from this journey into the microcosmic realms of matter reeling, intoxicated, ecstatic. But soon illusion had cast its veils upon her consciousness again, and she beat her hands against Krishna's breast as he tried to hold her close, shouting, "Unfaithful! Unfaithful! Unfaithful! Leave me alone and go, go away to all those others!"

Narada, slumped against a tree in Muthu Mohan's backyard, returned from his memory to the present, at once tired and consoled. No, Radha had never reconciled herself to Krishna's truth. Her human heart hadn't allowed her. But he, Narada, must be wiser than she. He must concede the truth of Vishnu's godhead that was far above and

19

beyond human reasoning. He, Narada, had achieved some measure of
enlightenment.

Narada now took some comfort in his superior wisdom. All right,
so Vishnu could visit Muthu Mohan's heart without compromising his
presence elsewhere. But his two-minute presence in the heart of this
"great devotee" did not make this devotee better than he, Narada.

Narada had seen Muthu Mohan through an entire cycle of his day.
There was nothing more he had to discover here. He now had to return
to Vishnu to let him know that he, Vishnu, was wrong.

Still a little subdued, Narada flew straight back to the Himalayas
in the north of India. It was dawn, and the day had not yet begun. He
strung his lute and sang the same song he had sung at the beginning of
this story, but this time the melody was sad and full of longing. When
he finished, he saw Vishnu, one leg on the other knee, leaning forward,
and smiling at Narada.

All Narada's anger surged up in him and he said, "Muthu Mohan
is not a better devotee than I! I witnessed all his life and thoughts and
except for that little, two-minute prayer . . ."

"Narada, what do you know of time?"

". . . two minutes, just two minutes!"

"Narada, it is not what you think. Two minutes is . . ."

"Two minutes is two minutes."

"Even a second with me, Narada, is eternity."

"Yes, I concede it wasn't a second," he said, not listening very well.
"And I concede that the prayer was, well, sincere, I can say that in all
honesty. But . . . but, not enough, not nearly enough to make him superior to me in any way whatsoever. I don't know what you are talking
about at all. I wake up every morning . . ."

". . . late," said Vishnu.

"All right! Late! What do you expect? I go to bed late, because I am
too busy singing to you. I sing to you all day long and at least half the
night!"

"More to hear your own voice, Narada, than to praise me."

"How can you say that? It isn't true. I don't know what's wrong with
you, but put me through any test. Any! And you'll see how sincerely
I am connected to you. Much more than Muthu Mohan, that 'great
devotee' of yours."

"Here, Narada," said Vishnu, producing a bowl full to the brim with
oil, with a wick in it, burning. "Put this on your head and circumambu-

late the city without spilling any of it or letting the flame go out. The rules are: no miracles, no flying through the air, no shortcuts. Let your feet touch the earth at all times, and put one foot before the other."

"Easy! Done!" said Narada, snapping his fingers, then holding the bowl with his hands, and placing it carefully on his head.

"Some test," thought Narada. "I can't imagine anything easier. I'm sure to succeed in this."

Well, Narada found it harder than he had thought, for often his heart and mind would stray into this or that, mainly the knot of his feelings about the entire Muthu Mohan affair, or the convoluted dialogue in his head, and then he would lose his balance, and almost trip. It was very difficult staying focused on the task at hand and utterly present. And then, as expected, all the winds and gales blew furiously, lashing poor Narada as he went about his trial. But Narada was an old rishi, an inspired sage and poet of the highest order, a son of Brahma himself, and all his practice and austerities saw him through this test. It took him all day to circumambulate the city, and when he arrived at the exact spot where he had started, Vishnu was waiting for him.

"There," said Narada, handing the bowl, with the flame still dancing in it, to Vishnu. "I've done it. And without spilling a drop. Not a drop, not even half a drop, not even a millionth of a drop did I spill. I have passed your test."

"And how many times," asked Vishnu, "did you think of me? Remember me?"

"Think of you! Remember you? Why, all my energy and concentration went into making sure I didn't spill a drop of that oil. Where did I have the time to think of you?"

Narada looked at Vishnu and without Vishnu saying a word, Narada understood with a flash of insight why Muthu Mohan was indeed a better devotee that he. Even though burdened with tasks as demanding as carrying the oil of his responsibilities on his head, he fulfilled them all with presence of mind, and remembered to remember Vishnu.

Narada fell at Vishnu's feet, feeling them against the skin of his cheek, and washing them with his tears.

"Forgive me," he whispered.

"Come, Narada," Vishnu said, lifting him up, and wiping his tears. "And now it is time for you to learn something about time. Come, pick up your lute. We have a journey to make."

ENTIRELY ENTANGLED

O ishnu and Narada, in their adventures in and out of eternity, had just left the cottage of a family who had fed and sheltered them for a night. In every direction, glistening desert dunes stretched out to the horizon.

"A more miserable family than this I have never met. Why," Narada asked Vishnu, "are human beings so blind and incapable of seeing themselves? In that home each one of them is suffering for no reason at all. The grandmother, who has lost her eyesight after years of weeping for a dead son, could easily have avoided it. Why do humans mourn at death when they have their entire lives to prepare for it? Tears are not going to bring him back to life. Besides, she has five others! And what a miserable bunch they are! The wives don't get along, the husbands are forever fighting over their father's property, and even though they have plenty, they don't think they have enough. I've entered all their thoughts and found not one—not even the children—to be happy. How can people be so foolish?"

"Compassion, Narada, compassion," Vishnu said. "This is the burden of being human, and none may escape it."

"I have escaped it. And I am not saying this out of pride," Narada said quickly, priding himself on his ability to catch thoughts that might sound arrogant to others. Yes, Narada was well versed in the sacred imperative of humility. "Certainly I grew jealous when I believed your love for other devotees exceeded your love for me, but it won't happen again. I have always cultivated the wisdom that you have taught me: do your best, and don't get attached to the fruits of your action. I stay anchored in detachment because I am conscious of my own inner processes. I have learned how to stay above emotions that are dead ends. My devotion to you, my meditations and music have all taught me to witness the drama of myself and of life around me. I am the bird that watches. You know that story, or shall I tell you?"

It often happened that when Narada spent long periods of time with Vishnu, the veils of familiarity obscured Vishnu's godhood from him and deluded him into thinking Vishnu was merely a close companion and a very good friend.

"Tell me, Narada, my teller of tales," Vishnu said, looking into Narada's eyes with amusement. As Narada stared back into Vishnu's eyes, he felt himself drawn to them like a bee to a flower, his entire being vibrating to the kind of ecstasy in which words cease and the earth stands still upon its axis. All around them the desert shimmered in the noon light, the heat rising in undulating waves above the sand. So still it became that even Narada's heart stopped beating while the two of them communicated through a thick plasma of silence.

Vishnu looked away, broke the spell, and sat down on a boulder, one foot on top of the other knee. He kneeled forward, and repeated his request.

"Tell me the story of the bird."

"Birds . . ." Narada said, shaking himself and trying to regain his reason, which always offered him a sense of comfort and safety. "There are two birds on the Tree of Life."

"Are you sure, Narada? I thought there was only one."

"No, no. Two. Definitely two. One of them sits at the very top of the tree and witnesses the goings-on around him. Now this reminds me of another story, but I will wait to tell you that one till I have finished this one. Stories, Vishnu, are like snarled threads, each connected with the other, and it's very tempting to want to tell them all at once. But time, linear, progressive, maddening time, won't let me."

"Are you sure time is linear, Narada? Just yesterday," Vishnu said, picking up a thin sliver of petrified wood from the sand, "this desert was a thick forest, so thick no light could shine through on the forest floor."

"Yesterday? It was eons ago, surely."

"No, yesterday. And the day before it was an ocean with roaring waters," Vishnu said, unearthing a spiral shell with his toe.

"Time is undoubtedly linear," Narada repeated, a little bit annoyed with Vishnu for all his interruptions. "Words follow one after another in a line. Words, sentences, paragraphs, pages, sense, all unfold in time, like a seed planted in the earth takes time to grow into itself. So, since time is linear, I will draw out just one single strand and not risk losing my audience. The bird that watches, Vishnu, is the yogi, the ascetic bird, all his senses drawn in and therefore immovable by desire. The other one is the bhogi, the sensual experiencer, taster of life, one who enjoys the fruits of the tree, eating and nesting, laying eggs, hatching her young, and so on. I, Vishnu, am the bird that watches and witnesses."

"Are you certain?" Vishnu asked.

"You surprise me, Vishnu. Have I ever married? Have I ever fallen in love? No, no, none of that is for me. Sexual love seduces humans with its magic and illusion. That is why Narada is celibate. Human, sexual love is the root of delusion and attachment. Ah, Narada needs none of it. Narada loves his lute," he said, strumming it, hugging its body, kissing its blow hole with loud smacks.

"Don't be too certain, Narada. Love is the sweetest dream. Even gods succumb to love. Even I, who love to sleep and dream, have surrendered to it many times. Once, when I went to rescue Earth when she sank beneath the primal sea, she wrapped her arms around me helplessly and looked into my eyes with that look which cannot be described. I was ravished and enchanted by her. I spent thousands of years as a pig, loving and being attached to all my joys and sufferings. I would still be there if Shiva hadn't killed me with his trident. Once, in yet another incarnation, as Rama, I loved Sita dearly, and was very distraught when Ravana abducted her. And then, of course, you know all my exploits as Krishna. Love, Narada, is the magic of Maya. I will tell you more: I made love to Maya, as well, and begot time."

The mention of his many reincarnations reminded Narada of Vishnu's godhood, and he wondered for a moment if he had taken too many liberties with his friend.

"What is this Maya, Lord?"

"It is illusion, Narada. This three-dimensional world looks solid and convincing, but it isn't really there. It is as insubstantial as a dream. See?" asked Vishnu, passing his hand through Narada as if the musician was made of air. Luminous molecules, dancing particles swarmed out of and into him.

"But that's because we are immortals," Narada protested.

"No. This pertains to everyone. Everything."

"I can't quite grasp the idea of Maya. Could you put it in a comprehensible formula for me, Lord Vishnu?"

"Maya is the illusion by which the One supreme force appears as the many. She is the great weaver who sits in the center of her web, weaving it and ensnaring her victims in its golden threads. It is the great force that is the very glue of life, Narada. Very few, one in a trillion, perhaps, escape the phantasms of Maya."

"Could you be a little more explicit, please?"

"I am thirsty, Narada. Here, fetch me some water in this gourd from that river."

Narada turned around, and sure enough, right there in the desert meandered a wide and fast-flowing river that wasn't there the last time he had looked about him. He wondered if Maya meant "magic."

"Here—fetch the water from the middle of the river. It is sweetest, clearest, and coolest there."

Narada took the proffered container, and leaving his lute leaning on the dune where Vishnu sat, walked to the river, marveling at how an entire river had appeared to quench Vishnu's thirst.

Narada stepped into the swiftly moving river, its currents lashing his feet and ankles. Remembering Vishnu's injunction to fetch the water from the middle of the river, he waded in further, till the waters reached his waist. Narada thought he heard Vishnu say something, but the rapids were so loud that Narada couldn't make out the words. By the time he reached the middle, Narada was sucked downward by an eddy so powerful that he lost all control. He spun rapidly round and round in tumultuous circles, swirling and whirling till all Narada had known before was dislodged and washed out of his skull. He forgot who he was, what he was doing there, where he had come from, or where he was going. Even his body melted away in the waters and just a microscopic, tadpole-like creature remained.

Narada's being sensed a radiant corona before him, and swam towards it furiously, propelled by a purpose he couldn't comprehend. He knew only that his life depended on it and he had to get to it to survive. His tiny head pierced through the transparent, numinous membrane of the halo, entered it, and swam towards its center.

A translucent cloud of water surrounded him. All was still and quiet inside. Floating freely in a warm, fluid-filled cavity, his being fell into a sweet slumber. And in this sleep he grew, like a fetus in a womb, developing all his sense organs, his spine, heart, and other organs.

From this sleep Narada was awakened by pulsing contractions. His head rotated, slithered downwards through a canal, engaged in a bony structure, and gradually, emerged on soft sands amidst the breaking of waters.

He came to consciousness on the banks of the river. Someone was crying, and upon opening his eyes he saw that it was himself. He rolled over and stood on all fours, cleared the fluid from his nose and mouth, then got unsteadily to his feet.

"Who am I? Where am I? What am I doing here in this desert? Where did I come from?" He asked himself a succession of questions with no answers. No trace of a memory remained. The only thing he knew was that he was ravenously hungry. He looked around and saw, just a short distance away, a town with dome-like wooden houses and mud huts. People jostled about in the streets, children played, and cows and bulls roamed on the outskirts, in the desert, grazing on the meager shrubbery. None of it looked familiar. It was all new and very strange.

He was compelled to move towards one of the wooden houses in town. As he neared it, he heard sounds of keening and wailing inside. The door opened, and a woman cried out, "Bimla, Dev Dutt is here!"

He thought to himself, "so, that's my name: Dev Dutt."

A young woman in a white sari came to the door. He had never seen her before, yet when he looked into her eyes, he felt he had known her for all time. A memory stirred within him of other, familiar eyes, like lotuses in deep, dark pools which made him long to submerge in them. And as the woman gazed back, her eyes love-filled, alluring, the desert all around him sprang alive in an instant. Trees grew and blossomed with fragrant flowers, a soft, cool breeze sprang up, caressing his limbs, and birds began to sing sweetly. The desert vanished and Earth became paradise.

Bimla took him by the hand and brought him inside, where a shrouded body lay stretched upon the ground. Dev Dutt knew without words that this was the body of her father. He also knew that he was destined to take his place as the head of the family.

Bimla sat him down on the floor and fed him from the funeral feast. Dev Dutt ate as if he had never, ever eaten before. Everything tasted new and delicious. The buds of his tongue sang with pleasure at all the plethora of dishes and delicacies. Sour and salty, bitter and sweet all melded together to form an exquisite sensation. And every now and then, Dev Dutt and Bimla looked into each others' eyes, and feasted on the sight of each other.

The days followed in quick succession after the funeral. Dev Dutt asked Bimla to marry him, she consented, and her mother gave her consent as well. The marriage ceremony over, Dev Dutt began to enjoy connubial bliss. The buds of all his senses bloomed. He took pleasure in the sight of his wife moving about the hut, the feel and touch of her at night. He delighted in the musky odors of her skin, the aromas from the kitchen, the incense from the altars, the fragrance of the flowers, the taste of wine. The sound of her voice, the roar of the river's water, the wind, the babble and laughter around him, and the songs of street musicians resounded in the labyrinths of his ear. It was the sound of music, above all else, that stirred him and connected him to someone, something that he couldn't name.

Dev Dutt took over the family fields and labored hard to make them yield their crops. Soon, the conception of a child was announced, filling him with small waves of joy as he moved through his days, working and eating and touching his wife's belly in love and gratitude. When he looked at Bimla's eyes now, it wasn't just the two of them that were joined together with the filaments of love, but three. And not just three—the coming of this child made them feel their connection with the entire created world, its miracles and mysteries. They were bound to it all by threads of light. Even as the child grew in her mother's womb, tentacles of attachment grew from Dev Dutt's heart and wrapped themselves around her. He walked about full of gratitude and a heightened sense of grace. And though he still didn't know who he was, where he came from, it didn't matter. Life was on course. Everything was as it ought to be, perfect and unimaginably sweet

During Bimla's pregnancy, the price of grain went up and Dev Dutt made a great deal of money with which he bought a bigger house for his growing family. He bought bulls and cows, hired many servants and farm hands, and started a new business selling yogurt, milk, cheese, and ghee.

The child arrived, a lovely girl whom they named Chandini. And when she was old enough to open her eyes, Dev Dutt saw that she, too, had very familiar eyes, the eyes that reminded him of something or someone he couldn't name or remember. Chandini's eyes, too, enchanted and enmeshed him.

Dev Dutt soon became the richest man in town. All his family's material wants were satisfied. He spent a great deal of time making, spending, counting, and saving his money. At the same time, he sought prestige and power and became the head of the panchayat, the local political body. He was honored and admired, respected and envied.

More children came: a son, Guru Dutt, another daughter, Roshini, and then another daughter, Ujjala. The chords of his heart wrapped around all of them tightly. He got involved in their upraising and education, and as time streamed away, their marriages as well. Grandchildren came—all with the same eyes that reminded him of something he couldn't name. And though indeed every one in the village had the same eyes, Dev Dutt saw only the eyes of his family.

He still loved his wife dearly. Passion turned into companionship, then friendship. Together they delighted in their grandchildren, united in their concern for each other and the well-being of the family fabric, held together with the fibers of attachment.

Through the recurring seasons, Dev Dutt's life settled into the usual circle of ups and downs within the wheel of time. He hoped for a good monsoon, and despaired when it didn't come in time; he was elated when he could negotiate a good sale of his products in the next town, and depressed when some unpredictable disease devastated his stock; he worried when any family member fell sick, and rejoiced when all were healthy and happy.

But one day, the course of Dev Dutt's life changed suddenly and dramatically. Heavy monsoons made the river flood. Each day his family watched the river swell in the heavy deluge. They hoped the deluge would abate, and despaired that it wouldn't. As the days passed, the very foundations of the house were undermined by the water. One night it groaned and shook like a cardboard box. Dev Dutt and Guru Dutt managed to get everyone out of the house in time, but the house itself broke apart, its fragments floating away like paper boats in a stream.

With a grandchild perched on each shoulder, and his hand clutching his wife's hand, Dev Dutt made his way through the waters, slipping and sliding on the mud beneath his feet. In the distance he saw Chandini and Roshini twirling in a whirlpool. He cried out to them, extending an arm, but they were gone. The movement made one grandchild slip off his shoulder and fall. Dev Dutt watched helplessly as she swirled in the waters and disappeared. He wept and cried aloud hopelessly, add-

ing his own flood of tears to the rain. Further downstream he saw his son and daughter, Guru Dutt and Ujjala, too, washed away like logs in the current. The despair in his heart weakened his aged body, and he stumbled, dropping his other grandchild into the river, and loosening his grip on his wife's hand. His heart desolate with grief, he saw all the members of his family drift away from him before he, too, lost his footing and fell into the turbid flow, wheeling and revolving in the flood.

"I don't want to die! I don't want to die," he kept repeating. "I want to live and reunite with my family!"

He felt himself rushing through a dark tunnel and knew that this was the end, this was death. Despair gripped his heart tightly as he tumbled headlong in the waves.

"Narada," he heard a voice say just as he was beginning to lose consciousness. "Narada, don't get the water from the middle . . ."

Hearing the voice, Dev Dutt found himself on solid ground. He opened his eyes and saw that he was standing a third of the way into the river, facing the middle. He saw houses drift by, and bodies he recognized as the bodies of people he loved. He gasped in shock when he recognized one of the bodies as his own. Turning toward the bank, he saw the desert shimmering in the sunlight, and a figure, wholly familiar, entirely new, sitting upon a boulder, looking at him.

". . . where you are is deep enough," Vishnu said.

Narada shook himself, like a dog shakes himself after being submerged in water. And all the drops flew off him—a shower of droplets, each a little bubble of an entire lifetime. He looked down at his hand and saw that he held a gourd full of water. Still reeling from his life and death, still uncertain about who he was and what had happened, he walked towards the figure on the boulder. Ah! Now he remembered what it was that he couldn't remember or name: Vishnu!

All the eyes that he, Narada as Dev Dutt, had loved in his lifetime that had lasted a split second had been Vishnu's! He it was who had divided and multiplied himself into the many. And now they had all returned to their origin in Vishnu's body. Maya was all Vishnu's lila, a play, a dance in illusory duration whose causal cycles and gyres seemed endless but were no more than tiny blips in eternity.

Vishnu held out his hand for the gourd, took it, and smiling over the rim, took a nice, long draft. Then he lowered it, and said, "Maya is a long sleep and a forgetting, Narada. Blessed are the people who are awake."

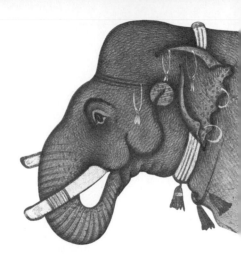

Vishnu Forgets

*W*hen Earth, weighted down by ignorance, sunk to the bottom of the cosmic ocean, it was Vishnu that incarnated as Varaha, the Boar, to rescue her. He dove into the ocean, nosed his way to the darkest and deepest region, where Earth lay on the verge of dissolution, and carried her up from the murky depths. As he arose again, Earth put her arms around him, looked into his eyes with love and gratitude, and spoke.

"My Lord, O how many times have you rescued me thus?"

Vishnu, who had been rather annoyed with her for having disturbed his peace, nevertheless fell in love with her instantly. He hadn't meant to. It was quite contrary to his intention and his mission: to recover the sunken Vedas—holy books, repository of the wisdom of the ages— which along with Earth had sunk to the bottom of the primeval sea. Vishnu had intended to set her afloat in the cosmos so she could birth and support life again, and return to his exalted position as the first of gods. But now, enraptured by Earth's embrace, he didn't want to return to Vaikunth, the home of the gods.

And this really annoyed Shiva. It offended his sense of how a god the stature of Vishnu should behave. Here was Vishnu, fleeing from his responsibilities, feeding, fighting, fornicating in the mud with Earth, who had assumed the form of a sow to mate with her Lord's incarnation as a boar. Enamored and ensnared by the illusion of life, he had forgotten his true nature. Shiva knew that other tasks, other heroic incarnations awaited Vishnu. His godhood and bliss awaited him.

Shiva decided to pay a visit to Varaha in order to wean him away from his porcine passions. Shiva reached his destination in the heat of the morning. Varaha, caked with the mud in which he had been wallowing, snorted through a pungent garbage heap.

"Varaha, it is time to return," said Shiva, keeping a safe distance from the filthy beast.

Varaha lifted his head, looked at Shiva through his hairy eyeballs, grunted, and returned to swilling his slop. It tasted so delicious he refused to be disturbed.

"There is more to life than your tongue, Varaha!"

"What does the ascetic Shiva know about taste?" Varaha thought, and continued to slurp and snort.

"You obtuse, inarticulate beast! You are too besotted with this illusion to remember your true form! You are the eternal flame of God!"

Varaha waddled over to his piglet, touched her snout with his own, and bellowed in delight. The piglet ran away playfully, and began to tug at her mother's teats. Varaha rolled some more in the mud, then nuzzled near his mate, and fell asleep.

"I have to go talk to Brahma, and make him speak to Varaha's soul, tell him to abandon his earthly form—which is but the reflection of a reflection, a shadow, a shade—and return to Vaikunth," Shiva thought.

Varaha, who opened one sleepy eye, was relieved to see Shiva go. "What does Shiva, always looking to destroy, know of the joys of being?" thought Varaha. "What does he know of the peace that comes after striving is laid to rest? Haven't I done more than my share of work? Haven't I just finished the mammoth task of rescuing Earth from drowning? Shiva would have me keep moving on and on. What does he know of the sweetness of a life beyond conflict? What can be better than playing in the mud with your mate? I could live for eternity in its warm comfort, feeling my mate's hide next to mine while my piglets chase each other and fall all over us. But that Shiva is not going to let me rest. It's best to go into hiding."

Varaha took his family and fled into the jungles of the Himalayas. There he became enthralled with the beauty of the mountains, the deodar trees, and the flowing water outside his cave. His mate and offspring lived well and thrived. No, he wasn't ready to leave this life just yet.

Meanwhile, a desperate Shiva went to Brahma. "Lord, Vishnu, as Varaha, is miserably attached to his existence—to rutting and spawn-

35

ing, grunting and groaning, attached even to the garbage heaps of India, routing about in them with his snout and face caked with mud. He is content just to be with and in the Earth, who, now a sow, lies there amidst the filth, suckling her young. Lord, let Varaha know that it is time for him to abandon his boar form, and return to carry out his sacred tasks."

"Of course, of course. You are right, my dear Shiva. Attachment is not to be tolerated. I will do this in all haste," Brahma replied.

But as soon as Shiva left, Brahma fell into a quandary. Though he knew Shiva was right, he didn't feel like getting Varaha to abandon Earth just yet. He was indulgent of life and all its twisted, colorful variety. "That Shiva is in one of his ascetic phases and thinks everyone should do as he does, or rather, doesn't do," he thought. "Varaha is so content. Let him be that way a bit longer. Let Shiva concern himself with something more than the pleasures of a pig. More than a few earthly leaders are acting worse than Varaha these days. Let Shiva go destroy their lives."

But Shiva, frustrated and fretting, grew tired of waiting for Brahma to do something, and decided to take matters into his own hands. He had no trouble finding Varaha in his mountain hideout. And though Varaha saw Shiva coming and made ready to flee, this time Shiva wasn't attacking with mere words. Shiva let his trident fly at the galloping boar. And when Shiva shoots his trident, there is no escaping it.

His life ebbing out of him in carmine spurts, the fatally wounded Varaha opened his eyes in final reflection: "How beautiful my blood is. How magnificent the green trees, the stream singing upon the boulders, my lovely wife, my sweet little piglets, my home, my body, my white tusks, my beautiful bristles, my broad and hairy feet. Ah, how beautiful is this web that I am entangled in! How beautiful, and now, how painful. Ah, the pain. How I love even the dregs of this illusion: pleasure and pain, joy and sorrow, life and death. Death? Is this the end? Nothing? Oblivion? Mud into mud?"

"Oh Varaha!" cried Shiva, his strident voice hitting the slackening drums of Varaha's ears: "Relinquish 'me' and 'mine'! Let go of doubt! It is time for you to leave this illusion and return to your true nature. Remember who you are. Remember that you are spirit, Vishnu, the undying, formless energy of the universe. You are formless light, the eternal, undying flame."

"Have I really forgotten who I am? Am I truly Vishnu?" Varaha wondered, as the individual wave of his consciousness began to merge into a vast ocean of gentle light, ebbing and flowing in concentric circles to a low humming vibration.

"How marvelous my Earth is," he thought, taking a last look with his darkening, dimming vision. "How extraordinary! How sweet! I hope my beloved Earth needs rescuing every now and then, for there is nothing I would like better than to reincarnate again and again to be with her."

Out of Vishnu's Mouth

Saint Markandeya, the renowned and deeply respected sage, had a prodigious brain, a marvelous mind, great health, and happiness. A thousand years old, he came from a great lineage of wise men who possessed all the secrets of life. Markandeya's greatest revelation, which he propagated and preached far and wide with much success, was that he, and all of us, including all the creatures and the inanimate world—indeed, the entire known universe—exist within Vishnu's body as the god sleeps on the Cosmic Sea. The firmament is the globe of Vishnu's skull, the planets, stars and galaxies his thought, the sun his eye. Markandeya knew that Vishnu's silent mouth was the source of all sound, his throat and lungs the spring of all songs, his arteries and veins our river and streams, and Vishnu's heart the very pulse of the world.

In fact, the word "pulse" sent Markandeya into an ecstatic trance as he contemplated the rhythm of the universe. Everything that he could think of—and he could think of it all: the seasons, night and day, the phases of the moon and the ocean, the diastole and systole of nature—was rhythm regulated to some unheard, but everywhere visible, cosmic beat: the beat of Vishnu's heart.

"What a miraculous universe! How marvelously balanced and proportioned! How mathematically precise its underpinnings! How awesome the physiology of rivers and streams, wind and air! What harmony, from the cells in the body to the planetary spheres in their orbits whirling to the unheard sound of music!" Markandeya would wax poetic as he preached. "And you and I, all of us, are also notes in the great harmony of life! How stupendous it is, that we have been given the mind, the brain, the consciousness, the vision to see and know the intricacies of this universe's design!"

His devotees clapped and bowed, genuflected and adored him.

One day, as Markandeya was roaming about in Vishnu's mouth, as he was wont to do, contemplating the marvels of language, alphabets, words, and names, he suddenly tripped and found himself falling into a deep, watery abyss. The blue, cloudless sky darkened at noon. It wasn't just the clear darkness of a starless night, but there was a profound matte blackness, cold and frigid, that deeply confused Markandeya. He, who knew all the intricate workings of the universe, had never had such an experience before. He rubbed his eyes and pinched himself, but the void persisted in all directions, colorless, starless, unbounded, trackless abyss.

A violent wave, accompanied by a noisy, cacophonous sound, swept him up and he found himself swirling furiously in a vortex of water so powerful that he was like a twig in a maelstrom. Round and round and up and down he whirled, disoriented and afraid. All his knowledge about Vishnu, geometry, language, number, and image, melted in the waters in which he found himself immersed up to his chin. He was breathing through his mouth, in short, desperate gasps.

Neither Markandeya's intelligence nor his wisdom could help him fathom this experience. Where was he? How did he get here? Why did this happen? What was its meaning? Was he still in Vishnu's body? In his heart? Was Vishnu—oh, terror!—having a heart attack? What happened to the god in whose body he so safely roamed, delighting in its harmony and beauty, feeling the warm, comforting beat of Vishnu's heart in his ears?

And then suddenly his powerful mind sent him the insight that he had fallen out of Vishnu's mouth into the cosmic waters on which the god slept! The notion brought some comfort to Markandeya. But this soon dissipated, for try as he might, he couldn't see even the vague outline of the slumbering god.

Because Markandeya had been suddenly and unexplainably expelled from his home within Vishnu's body, his previous vision of harmony was like a fading dream inside his despairing and doubtful head. Words and thoughts began to fail him, and he seemed on the verge of death, for which he was not ready even after a thousand years of living. How could this be happening to him, Markandeya, the All-Knowing? And why? Surely there was a reason for it, which he would be able to grasp if only the roaring of this ocean would subside. But he thrashed about in the waters, like a drowning man who sees no shore.

Markandeya concentrated hard, recalling his austerities. He succeeded in clutching the thin straw of his will power, and clambering up on it. He visualized the body of Vishnu, and sure enough, the darkness abated a bit and he perceived the outline of the sleeping god again, half submerged, half floating on the waters. Markandeya concentrated harder, and in the faint light saw Vishnu's hand reach out for him, like a raft. Wet and shivering like a drowned rat, he scrambled up on it, climbed up the pores of Vishnu's cheeks precariously, before sliding into the gaping slit of Vishnu's mouth once again.

Ah! Once again Markandeya was in Vishnu's body and behold, his safe and familiar world was back! The sun shone in his soul, making the inner and outer territory numinous with light and color. His joy, his delight in everything external, and at his own inner mechanisms, the grace of an unclouded consciousness, the clear lens of his senses that allowed him to perceive the purpose of the world and himself in it, returned, anew, fresh, as if for the very first time.

And Markandeya's sermons changed with his new experience, which he incorporated into a slightly amended vision of the universe. From that time on, the sage preached that silence and emptiness, like a blank canvas or parchment, without which no words or forms could exist, were also part of reality; that chaos and cacophony were also part of the song of life. He would tell his followers that even though the world was measured, it wasn't mathematical and entirely predictable; that there were variations within regularity, oscillations in the order. After all, Vishnu did not lock himself within some rigid pattern, but was free to improvise.

But though Markandeya was still healthy and strong, his bliss was edged with doubt. He was no longer a happy man, for he had experienced the great void that surrounded the counterpoint of order and chaos in the cosmos. As he resumed his peregrinations in Vishnu's body, his brain was abuzz with questions. Was there nothing solid and substantial about the world as he knew it? What was it that made his experience oscillate from dark to light, thus? And what was real? This or that? Harmony or cacophony? Peace or that other experience that was not even amenable to or expressible in words? Could he choose to be in "this" which he understood and loved? This was safe, that was dangerous; this was life, which he loved and was attached to, and that was death, which he feared and never wanted to experience again.

So, for another thousand years, Markandeya worked with a great deal of effort and concentration to recreate his world as something more congenial and comprehensible, and succeeded. And once again his happiness was re-established. The sage continued to explore the geography of god's earth, the configurations of Vishnu's mind, wondering and musing, contemplating and meditating, preaching and teaching. Yet, just when he had forgotten his own death and thought he had figured existence out once more—"this" was real and the other just an aberration—Markandeya fell out of Vishnu's mouth again.

The sage went through the same dissolution of form and color, language and image, boundary and shape, the same inner and outer turmoil and agitation as before. But this time his brain and will failed him entirely. Nothing made any sense, his bank of knowledge showed up empty and utterly incapable of rescuing him. Markandeya was sinking rapidly, and was certain this was the end of his life. He was overcome with despair.

"Vishnu, save me, Vithala!" he cried out aloud from the depths of his desolate heart. "Give me your hand and pull me out of these turbulent, churning waters. Rescue me, Lord! Help me swim across this, and return to your safe shores! Markandeya knows nothing. Even his humility is pride!"

In a dim light, as in early dawn, Markandeya saw a child sleeping blissfully on the waves. For a moment he was stunned at the sight. But gradually, as was usual with Markandeya, his brain went rapidly into action. Who was this child? Where did it come from? How did it survive the dangerous ocean, and how could it be so trusting and unafraid?

The child awoke, stretched its luminous limbs, and began to dance within a shower of golden particles. It swam and cavorted in the sea, splashed about in the dark depths, scrambled up on the body, barely perceptible, of the sleeping God, plunged into the roiled waters, leaped into the air, entered and exited Vishnu's mouth at will, leaving a trail of gold dust, swirling and dancing, free and unfettered.

And as Markandeya marveled at the sight before him, his mind so benumbed by the creature's grace and fluidity that not a thought remained in it, the child came near Markandeya, clapped its hands, and said, "You!"

Markandeya, venerated, honored, worshipped sage, swelled in rage

41

at the child. In the light of his anger, the child appeared to him to be
just any rude and ill-mannered child. How dare it insult the honorable
sage with this rudeness! No one had ever called him "You!" before.
He was always the Ancient One, the Wise One, the Long-Lived One,
Saint Markandeya. Frustrated and furious, he gave chase to the child,
intending to catch and punish it, but the child, who seemed very close
to him, just laughed and remained ever beyond reach. As the little one
flicked its hands before Markandeya's face, from them poured a shower
of golden particles that enveloped him, coalesced into forms, images,
symbols, worlds, and ages, then scattered away like clouds, only to

return again—always changing, and always the same.

Markandeya's anger melted away in the shower of light all around
and within him. And when he looked at his hand, that too was insubstantial, pulsing like a formless energy field of light. He looked all
around himself and delighted as a child would in the visions before him,
mesmerized. But then his overactive brain, full of words and images,
began to plague him again, and he felt confused.

"Who are you, O child that plays thus in this terrifying cosmic
ocean? Tell me, why do I keep falling out of Vishnu's body?"

"Vishnu's body!" laughed the child. "What body?"

Markandeya looked and the thin outline of the sleeping god vanished
as if into thin air. And with its disappearance Markandeya knew with
some faculty beyond the intellect that Vishnu's body had been a construct of his own mind; that all his images were for his own comfort,
fabrications of the mind, illusions to keep him safe, veils to hide from
him the deep and unfathomable mystery of his own being in the world;
that the energy whose manifestation was the sleeping god, himself,
and the child, was deathless, without limits and dimensions, forms and

features, size or shape; that no name, image or metaphor could contain or explicate it entirely; that all his knowledge amounted to zero in the face of the mystery of the universe and of life.

The child curled up on the waters and fell asleep again. And as Markandeya watched it sleeping, a great love arose in the sage, a love that enveloped the child and himself, womb-like, in a golden glow. He picked up the child in his arms and held it close. He felt as a woman might feel who picks up her newborn, unable to distinguish between herself and it. His heart opened as a flower, unfurling undreamt of spaces, one within the other, endlessly. Markandeya had felt nothing like this before.

Markandeya held the child closer, but as he did, the child's limbs began to transform into wings, white as newly fallen snow, full of light, beating and fluttering against the walls of Markandeya's heart, opening it wider and wider. And there, before Markandeya's eyes, the child turned into a majestic gander, a swan, Parmahansa, Garuda, Vishnu's great bird, flapping its wings to the vibration of the wordless hum of the cosmos that creates, sustains, destroys, and creates ceaselessly.

Markandeya touched the bird, mounted it, and nestled into its feathers. The creature flew into the air, landed on the earth, returned to the ocean, swam on its surface, dived into the waters, reemerged, and flew into the sky, a pilgrim in all the elements, unfettered, homeless, and free.

And in its soft feathers, Markandeya slept a long, deep, and dreamless sleep.

When he awoke, the sage was safe in Vishnu's body once more, and it was morning. Birds were singing melodiously, the brooks were flowing, plants were flowering in all the colors of the rainbow, and clouds were sailing in the azure sky. And this time instead of wandering hither and yon, Markandeya made a small hut for himself on the banks of a stream in the Himalayas, and lived there quietly, resting, grateful for Vishnu's grace that allowed him to exist within the illusion of his dreams.

The saint chose to live out the rest of his life playfully, without being too attached to his ideas about the universe. He lived for many thousands of years in relative peace and harmony, knowing full well that everything was deathless, and love alone can bridge the abysses of the mind.

STORIES OF
BRAHMA

INTRODUCTION TO THE STORIES OF BRAHMA

Brahma, a member of the triad of principal gods of Hindu mythology, is the creator of the world, born in a lotus that springs out of Vishnu's navel as he sleeps on an undifferentiated, primordial ocean. Brahma was born with five heads, but lost one of them along the way to pride. While the world is Vishnu's dream, Brahma is the architect of that dream. Brahma fashions and populates the world with his mind-forms and also procreates humanity with his mate, the goddess Saraswati. The birth and dissolution of the universe is tied to the opening and shutting of Brahma's eyes. When the god's eyes open, a world comes into being that lasts for two billion, one hundred and sixty million years, and dissolves when Brahma shuts his eyes. Thus, according to Indian mythology, billions of worlds have come and gone, and are yet to come.

Indra, the lord of heaven, is also the god of fertility, rain and the atmosphere. Indra travels upon his mount, a white elephant called Airavata. Worshipped as a beneficent bestower of rain, Indra is also feared for the hurricanes, lightening and thunderbolts he hurls upon the earth and its demons. His arsenal includes the rainbow, which is his bow, and a magic net in which he catches his enemies. His reign lasts for a hundred heavenly years – equal to three hundred and sixty thousand earthly years -- after which another Indra succeeds him.

Indra is a very human god, susceptible to all the weaknesses of humankind: greed, rage, pride and lust. Indra is also addicted to soma, the divine nectar obtained by the gods when they churned the primeval ocean, and Form and Substance appeared out of the undistinguished chaos. Inebriated with soma, Indra goes off to war with his enemies: personified droughts that imprison the rains and winds, and characters like Ravana, the ten-headed demon king. Battling Ravana, Indra is defeated and imprisoned by Ravana's son, Meghananda, also known as Indrajit, or "conqueror of Indra."

How Brahma
Created the Dream

Brahma stirred, awoke, and stretched. He had just been born, and lay—still in the fetal position—on something soft and silken.

"Who am I? Where am I? Where did I come from, and what am I supposed to do here?" he said aloud, amazed at the mellifluous sound of his own voice.

To find answers to these questions, he opened his eyes, still sticky with prebirth mucous, and looked all around himself. A head with two eyes sprang up on the north side of his face. He stood up and looked with intensity in that direction, but he saw nothing but a dark void. There were no answers to his questions in the north. Another head sprang up on the south, with two more eyes to investigate his world. These eyes saw nothing in the south, and his questions remained unanswered. Three more heads, one to the east, west, and skyward, with two eyes each, failed to enlighten him. He became agitated, and felt utterly lost.

He sat down again, shut his eyes, and a thought swam into his soul. "I know I am made to create something, someone, but who and what? I cannot create in this darkness, and I cannot create without knowing who, what, or where I am."

He put his brains, which accounted for a large percentage of his body mass, to work. All his five heads fired billions of neurons; the electrical and chemical impulses traveled through the lobes and labyrinths, grey and white matter, convolutions and ganglia of his brain, but with no result.

He resolved, instead of looking outward and far away for answers, to look for them near at hand. As soon as he opened wide all ten eyes, they were flooded with a bright, scarlet light. He found himself surrounded by thin filaments in a corolla comprised of silken layers of diaphanous, veined, red tissue. Brahma reached out his hands and touched the soft velvety material surrounding him.

He stood up and peeped over the rim to see wide, green, waxy surfaces beneath him. Upon them rolled orbs of dewdrops refracting a thousand colors in the morning light, and beneath them rolled dark, onyx waters, undulating gently.

He looked all around again, north, south, east, west, and all the directions in between, including above and below, to catch a glimpse of anything else that was visible. But all he saw was a grey and even light, unbroken by any object.

He sat down and named his experience: "I am in a flower called a red lotus that is floating on water."

He now understood part of the enigma, but not enough to get him started on his tasks, which he was eager to perform. And while Brahma suspected the immensity of his potential and his power, he was still in the dark about what to do with it.

"Surely there is something on which this flower rests—and I'm going to find out what. Since I cannot discover anything about my origins from externals, I will investigate my immediate surroundings. I will descend into the lotus to discover what I can about myself. Thus far there is only one thing of which I am certain: I am."

He liked the thought very much, and repeated it silently. "I am. I am."

"Mantra," he said aloud, naming it.

He crossed his legs, sat like a lotus within the lotus, and with his mantra resounding in his consciousness, he embarked on his journey to himself.

Right beneath where he sat in the lotus, he saw a green, glowing orifice, like the mouth of a tunnel. He closed his eyes, repeated his mantra, and slid down the thin stalk, all his heads folding up like flower petals in the evening. Down the pistil he slid, gentle washes of color flashing on his eyelids: tangerine, canary yellow, brilliant green. Slipping gently down the constricted passage, past nodes and knots, Brahma was sometimes tempted to burst out into pointless activity and talk, but he continued to breathe his way down till he arrived at a large, blue chamber, the receptacle of the flower. Here the god sat for a long time, tasting bliss with his five tongues and every nerve and pore of his brain and body. With time he grew so still and silent that all his questions disappeared. Instead, he experienced the infinite spaces of his mind in which wheeled luminous, spiral galaxies with colorful cosmic dust and clouds, and nebula strewn with glinting, newly birthed stars.

But Brahma's destiny would not allow him to be content with bliss. He knew he was fated to act, to create all life in the universe: human, animal, plant, and mineral. He also knew he couldn't do this till he had discovered his origin, the source of his life and strength. And so, Brahma's restless urge to do propelled him to proceed further down the flower, from the lotus's receptacle, to the petiole and pedicel. Brahma traveled down, further down, through the flower stalk, waving and swaying in the waters, and downward still through the tap root to the dense, fibrous root system, before slithering out of the tip of a root into a purple soup of mud and water.

He swam about in the undulant, violet liquid to the sound of a low hum, a vibration made visible in the ripples and concentric circles of water reaching to the edge of the banks of the pool, and returning to the origin at the center. This sound, Brahma knew, was the source of energy that had created the flower that had birthed him. "Ah. But to what is this root attached?" he asked.

He dived into the waters in which he had been floating, and saw that the root went down into a round hole with folds of skin very similar to a hole with folds of skin in the center of his own body. "Navel," he named it aloud.

Head first, he slid down the slick surface of the umbilicus, which was also the root of the lotus, in through the navel. All was still and silent. Brahma was bathed in an ultraviolet light so gentle and soft that he felt himself nodding off to sleep. But not wanting to sleep, he gently repeated his mantra, "I am," till he became fully lucid again.

When Brahma opened his eyes he saw . . . nothing at first. Slowly, however, his eyes adjusted to the light, and he saw a sight that made him speechless. His newly acquired power to name utterly failed him; his newly formed brains were awed into silence. All words, definitions, descriptions, images, and metaphors abandoned the Lord of Language. He knew he would forever be unable to tell about this experience.

After a long spell of speechlessness, a name arose from the depths of him, a bubble of air that broke upon his tongue, dispersing amrita, the nectar of the gods, into his consciousness and his body: "Narayana. Narayana. Narayana: Lord of the Universe." And following that one name, others flowed through his mind:

Vishnu: He Who Is Everywhere and Pervades All Things.
Vishva: He Who Is Everything.
Bhuta-Krit: Maker of All Beings.
Bhuta-Bhrit: The Support of All Creatures.
Param-Atma: The Supreme Self.
Eka: The One.
Naika: The Many.
Aprameya: The Immeasurable.
Shanti-Da: Giver of Peace.

And so Brahma chanted, a string of a million billion names for this One who had no name.

Brahma knew that names would be central to the world that he was on the verge of creating. Names would be the warp and the weft upon which he would create the universe. Without names, nothing could be. And out of the million names that presented themselves to Brahma, the name that he picked for his experience of the primeval being who lay upon the waters was the first to roll off his lips: Narayana.

A long time Brahma stayed in this ultraviolet space, torn between his bliss and his activity, samadhi and samsara, eternity and duration, silence and speech. But then a thought convinced him to return back up again. "Vishnu is the matrix from which I was born and to which I will return. I can return to him anytime on the wings of my mantra. I am connected to Narayana with an umbilicus that cannot be severed. Connected and contained within him, I am he, substance of his substance, tissue of his tissue, breath of his breath, consciousness of his consciousness. As shall be everything I create."

With his attention firmly and forever rooted in this Reality, Brahma began his ascent up the lotus again to create the Dream of the World. From formless, incorporeal eternity, he rose up through violet, true blue, neon green, yellow, and orange, back to the scarlet of the lotus.

He sat for a while in the pool of nectar of the lotus, tasting the ecstasy of his senses. He knew then that though he could create many things and beings with his mind alone, he could not people the world without a mate.

No sooner had he articulated this thought than a longing arose in him which found its echo in a distant spring in the mountains. It began bubbling, frothing up through the earth, scattering boulders in the air as it burst forth like a fountain and began to flow rapidly, a vast and irrepressible river that bounded towards its destination: the ocean of Brahma's heart.

"Saraswati," Brahma said aloud, as she emptied into him. And as soon as he named her, she embodied as an ineffably beautiful woman, holding a flower in one of her four hands. In her second hand she held a blank book of palm leaves, in the third a damaru, a small drum with which to summon the rhythm-bound world, and in the fourth the vina, a stringed instrument, which she played as the background music to create the work of art called life.

Saraswati, Brahma's muse, inventor of the alphabet, maker of music, mother of the Vedas, patroness of poetry, goddess of all wisdom and science, architect of speech, was the one to give form to Brahma's thoughts. There amidst the stamens and the sepals, the pistils and the pollen in the petals, they made glorious love, and delighted in weaving Vishnu's plasma of golden particles into the solid matter of this so very insubstantial, crystalline, colored world.

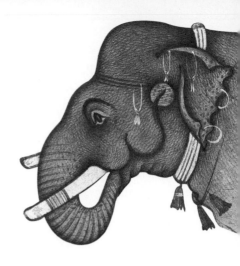

INDRA GETS CAUGHT

"You called?" Brahma asked, appearing before Indra, who lay bound, hand and foot, in the dungeon of the demon king, Ravana.

"Of course I called you, you stupid old fool," raged Indra. "Do you have eyes to see what Ravana has done to me?"

"I see," Brahma smiled calmly, sitting cross-legged on the thousand-petaled lotus that hovered a little above the dirt floor of the prison cell.

"So, is this the reward I get for fighting the Battle of Heaven, for confronting Ravana, the demon king?" Indra fumed, rattling the heavy chains that fettered his long hands and feet.

"Lord of the Rain, let anger go," Brahma replied.

"Let anger go? Don't I have cause to be angry? When Ravana came to my gate and demanded I surrender to him, did I not draw my silver sword and brighten the darkness? Did I not take a sip of soma, the ambrosia of the gods, and swear not to take orders from that dark and evil Ravana? I was the only god that challenged him. Is this how you treat your defenders? What's the use of being a god? I have had no support from you, or from any of the other gods."

"Lord of Fertility, let bitterness go," Brahma smiled.

"Do I not have cause to be bitter? What kind of a god are you, anyway? Is there no justice in your world? All the other gods have allowed themselves to become Ravana's slaves. They have given up the fight and surrendered to the demon, this son-in-law of Maya, the deceptive

Artist and Architect of the Earth who weaves illusions of power and grandeur to ensnare even the best of us. Agni, the fire god, heats the stoves in Ravana's kitchen, and keeps him warm; Vayu, the wind, sweeps the courtyards of his palaces in Lanka; Varuna, Lord of Waters, supplies the wines for Ravana's tables; the Sun lights his halls, and the Moon his gardens. I alone have stood firm and resisted his seductions. And what's my reward? These shackles!"

"Defender of gods and humans, let pride go."

"Let pride go! What pride have I left here, groveling in Ravana's dungeon? Brahma, why did you allow Ravana's son, Meghananda, to capture me? Have you no control over your creation? All day you sit on your lotus, three steps away from the edge of the universe, and meditate. You are to blame, do you hear me? The only reason Ravana is so strong is because you granted the demon a boon of immortality. How could you accede when Ravana demanded: 'Brahma, let me be unslayable by every creature of Heaven and of the underworlds.' Are you mad? Can you truly be the Lord of Creation?"

"It was for the higher good of all. If I hadn't granted Ravana the boon, he would have burnt up the worlds with his dreadful will and austerities."

"But why must I suffer now? The pain from these chains and the wounds from the battle are excruciating."

"Lord of the Thunderbolt, let pain go."

"It's easy for you to say that, isn't it? Not only do you grant boons to demons, but for capturing me in the net of illusion, you have awarded Ravana's son, Meghananda, the title of Indrajit, Conqueror of Indra."

Brahma laughed a joyous laugh.

"You mock at my sorrow? If you were here, I would give you a swift kick, and send you flying off that lotus. You laugh at me? You stupid . . . ineffectual god. Be gone!"

"You have to admit Meghananda performed an admirable feat, Indra. He took your very own weapon—your magnificent net of illusion, woven with gossamer and filaments of silk—and with his mighty, muscular arms, cast it wide, glimmering like gold dust, right above you. And your eye, so entranced by its scintillating light, lured you towards it and your hand reached out for it. You were caught in the very net you caught mortals in! Oh Indra, how marvelous was its beauty, how unsurpassable! Do you blame your judgment for being clouded by it? Even the illusion is Narayana's design. Even this is all his play! So? You, too, the mighty Indra, were caught. Rage against yourself, Indra, not me. Rage against your own anger, pain, resentment, and pride, for these imprison you more than Ravana's dungeon and chains."

Having said this, Brahma vanished from Indra's sight in a shower of twinkling laughter. He went to Ravana's son, and said, "Indrajit, mighty conqueror of Indra, free Indra now. He has had enough suffering. Free him, and take something in return from me."

"Immortality," Indrajit replied without a thought.

"Prince, I can't give you that gift. I have already caused a lot of trouble by granting that wish indiscriminately. Ask for something else."

"Then give me the power of invisibility, that I may be able to attack through thoughts of despair, put out lights left unguarded, bind my enemies with strong, invisible ropes of illusion that seem real."

"Granted," said Brahma.

"Here's the key," said Indrajit, handing Brahma the key to the dungeon in which Indra sat, raging.

"No, thanks, I don't touch weapons," Brahma replied.

"Weapons?" said Indrajit.

"Weapons of your illusion, Indrajit," Brahma replied, shutting his eyes as he sat on the lotus, and going into meditation. Deep in trance, Brahma entered Indra's mind and removed the cobwebs of despair and fear. And then he planted in Indra's mind the thought by which he could free himself.

Tired and weary of struggling and rage, Indra sat down on the dirt floor and went into meditation. In the very depth of silence, the thought that Brahma had sent him floated into his mind: "I am free. I am free. I am free."

Indra, dimly at first, then growing louder, heard the sound of an elephant trumpeting. He opened his eyes and saw that his fetters had fallen from him. The prison walls had dissolved, and above him unbound blue skies bloomed. Airavata, the white elephant, hovered in the air, flapping his ears, and summoning his master to mount and fly away to the celestial holy city of Amaravati, where he could once again rest, rejuvenate, and prepare for yet another inevitable battle.

STORIES OF

SHIVA, PARVATI, AND GANESHA

Introduction to Stories of Shiva, Parvati, and Ganesha

Shiva, god of destruction and death, is the third main deity in Hindu mythology. Though his role involves inflicting physical death, Shiva's primary purpose is to destroy ignorance in all its forms: lust, rage, avarice, pride, attachment and all other ego-centered grasping that afflicts humankind. He destroys only to create anew.

In many ways Shiva is the most interesting of the gods: the contradictions we see elsewhere are magnified in him. Though the enemy of lust, Shiva is also the god of sexuality. He is worshipped throughout India as the lingam, symbol of the phallus. He enjoys ecstatic lovemaking with his wife, Shakti. Though peace-loving, he is also the Lord of Rage. Though occasionally violent, Shiva is also one of the most forgiving of all gods. He loves and protects fiercely those who pay him even the slightest attention. Although he is the god of death, haunting ghats (cremation grounds), smearing his body and face with the ashes of the dead, and wearing a garland of bones around his neck, Shiva is also Lord of the Dance of Creation. His dance at the center of the world, in every human heart, is a creation dance so beautiful that one who witnesses it is transformed forever.

In popular iconography Shiva's hair, piled on top of his head, is the source of the Ganges River. A crescent moon shines in his topknot, and he has three eyes, one in the middle of his forehead with which he incinerates all fettering passions. His body is blue, and around his throat coils a large cobra.

Shakti is Shiva's mate through all eternity. Shakti means "force," or "energy." She is the primeval and constant energy of the universe, the Mother of the World. Shakti manifests in different times and forms. Like Shiva, many aspects of her personality are contrary: she is both wanton and the eternal virgin; a lover and a warrior; and, like Shiva, both creator and destroyer. The couple were once united as one, before Brahma created the world and separated them. Since then, Shakti's quest has been to reunite with Shiva. Shiva and Shakti's love is passionate and conflicted, and the battle of the sexes rages between them. Shakti's reincarnations, and thus her names, are numerous. Sati and Parvati are the only ones that need concern us here.

Ganesha, son of Shiva and Parvati, is the star of Indian mythology. Popular with the masses, he is a big-bellied god with the body of a man and the head of an elephant. Ganesha has only one tusk, as he broke the other one and used it as a pen to transcribe the great epic the *Mahabharata*. A corpulent god, Ganesha's fat belly is full of gifts—spiritual and material—for humankind. If loved, respected, and honored, Ganesha grants all wishes and removes obstacles to success.

THE MARRIAGE OF
SHIVA AND PARVATI

Parvati, embodiment of Shakti, sat meditating for a thousand years in a remote region of the Himalayas. She ate and drank little, avoided company, kept still and silent, and was simply clad in deerskin and bark, her hair in matted locks.

Most male sages practiced austerities to gain control and power over someone, something, or to get some material goal: a son, a kingdom, weapons, or revenge. The purpose of Parvati's meditation practice was simple and singular: she wanted to reunite with the One from whom she had been separated through many incarnations.

As she meditated, the scroll of her history unrolled in her consciousness, and many scenes from her past lives replayed themselves in her mind. Parvati remembered the beginnings of the birth of her individual consciousness.

In the process of creating the world, Brahma manifested from his mouth a strange, indescribable, asexual, membranous, egg-like creature. Terrified by it because he could not recognize it, Brahma, in a fit of postpartum anxiety and fear, cried out: "Divide yourself!"

The creature split into its elements, two halves which soon assembled two bodies, a base pair, each with its own nucleus: male and female, Shiva and Shakti.

Parvati remembered how beautiful her other half appeared to her at that time. Shiva was resplendent in his beauty and strength. She was filled with awe and wonder at this being that had emerged out of her, who was at once the other and her self. She couldn't tell where one began and the other ended. She was filled with a great, permeating, engulfing desire to merge with him again.

She had moved towards her male half, both object and subject of her desires, compelled, utterly without volition, like an iron filing towards a lodestone. She had touched Shiva's liquid skin with the tips of her fingers and begun to melt back into him when she heard a loud beating on a drum, and Brahma's thunderous voice shouted,

"No! Stay divided!"

And with his big stick, Brahma had torn the gossamer fabric that surrounded them, ripping it apart. The sight of Shiva began to fade from her newly-birthed eyes – dimmer, dimmer, dimmer – and gone!

Parvati recalled how painful and terrible that separation was. She had found herself frightening alone on the edge of a universe too wide for comfort. All she wanted was to be in Shiva's arms once more, surrounded and penetrated by him.

After an eternity of desolation, she turned away from the place of their separation and her birth into duality, determined to seek and find Shiva, and return with him again to the original state of undivided and unconscious bliss.

Shiva, on the other hand, found the pain so unbearable that he instantly turned away from it into the arms of wisdom. He resolved to be in control, rather than allow himself to be mauled by desire and afflicted with longing. Wearing a garland of skulls, he set off to the mountains in the company of ghosts to meditate on death and control his erotic inclinations.

After many years of austerities, Shiva freed himself of desire, and, consequently, had no empathy for the follies of humankind. He became insufferable in his pride, and laughed derisively at the other gods—Brahma in particular, who often lost his senses in the presence of beautiful women. Shiva danced comically and lewdly to show humanity the shameful face of its lusts and passions. He boasted endlessly of being the only god who was not ensnared by earthly entanglements.

Shakti, on the other hand, kept herself open to the suffering caused by the separation, certain that this primeval division engendered all conflict and struggle in the world. Human beings failed to live together in love and harmony because their hearts were restless without the One. And her search for her soul mate became her primary endeavor throughout each of her many lives.

Before her incarnation as Parvati, Shakti was born as Sati. In her youth, Sati had read all the holy texts and became a scholar of the scriptures. But she soon realized that all her knowledge could not fill her soul's emptiness. One day, in the young woman's presence, a passerby mentioned the word "Shiva," sending Sati into a trance in which she tasted again the blissful unity she had forgotten. From then on, Shiva became the object of her longing. There was nothing else she wanted. She prayed, fasted, meditated, and sang songs to him.

Brahma was so impressed by her love and one-pointed devotion that he approached Shiva and asked him to take a wife. Shiva declined, and Brahma had to resort to a stratagem. Together with Sati, he brought Kama, God of Love, to Shiva. Kama shot an arrow into Shiva's heart at the precise moment he looked into Sati's eyes, and someone other than his conscious self drove Shiva to say, "Marry me!"

Parvati savored again in memory the fiery and gentle days of their courtship as Shiva and Sati. Fragments of a poem he had scribbled on bark leaf floated into her mind:

That girl! That girl! What wonder to depart from trance!
Precious fragrance drifts from her golden skin, mingles with smoky
Musk from my ashes, then lifts another petal from the golden lotus,
Pours the nectar of the Ganges over my hair, cleansing me from the ghats.

Parvati writhed with longing as she remembered their passionate wedding night. She felt herself drowning in the sweet density of desire, her body burning in love. "Oh Shiva," she cried in her meditation. "Shiva! Shiva! Shiva!"

As Parvati continued to relive her former life, she did not dwell long on Sati and Shiva's subsequent life together—which proved an unhappy one. Sati's father did not approve of her marrying Shiva, a crazy mendicant who did not believe in owning material possessions, took intoxicants, communed with the dead, and left his daughter to survive the elements (Shiva scorned living in a house, and the comforts that imprisoned one's soul.)

Instead, Parvati's thoughts sped past this history, avoiding recall of its tragic finale, in which Sati had committed suicide after her father insulted Shiva by not inviting him to his feast. Shiva had carried her body parts around, weeping and howling like an animal in pain.

In the early years of her present lifetime as Parvati, she did not meditate, believing that a love such as hers and Shiva's would find its fulfillment spontaneously. But Shiva did not come for her, and so she embarked upon the traditional austerities.

All those around her believed Parvati had renounced ordinary life when she went off to meditate in the mountains; not one knew that the purpose of her efforts was not to seek enlightenment or liberation, but to join with her Lord again! Nothing mattered to her except Shiva! Shiva! Shiva! Her heart leaped in its cage of bone at the very sound of his name.

"How many eons have we been separated?" Parvati thought, addressing herself to Shiva. "How terribly long it has been since I reunited with you, my dark Lord of the Lotus Eyes, felt your arms around me, and your entire being sheathed inside me?"

Opening her eyes for an instant, Parvati spied someone coming towards her on the mountain path. Could it be that her mate had heard the call of her heart? Could it be . . . Shiva? She rose and ran down to meet him, her eyes blurring with emotion. When she stood before the figure, however, Parvati was dreadfully disappointed to see he was only an aged beggar.

Struggling with her anguish, Parvati decided to converse with the old man anyway. She had been alone for a thousand years and was grateful in any case for the beggar's presence.

He opened his eyes wide in surprise at the sight before him. "Oh, lovely, beautiful woman, why are you practicing these austerities in the prime of life? Why is your hair not combed and braided with jasmine? Why have you set aside comforts and ornaments for matted hair, and discarded silken clothes for tree bark?"

"I am waiting for Shiva, holy one. Have you seen him anywhere?"

"Why are you waiting for him?"

"To make him my husband again."

"Your husband? Foolish girl, do you not know? Shiva wants nothing to do with women!"

"How dare you call me foolish?" Parvati replied, her fury surging. Darkness descended and black clouds formed in the sky.

"Calm down, beautiful woman. I just wanted to know how you could possibly want to marry that dirty fellow. He is the Lord of Ghosts, with ashes in his veins instead of blood. He dances wildly in the cremation grounds and smells of death. He drinks and eats out of a skull, sleeps with corpses, and wraps himself, when he is not naked, in the skins of the dead. You should know better than to want that mad fellow for a husband."

"How dare you call Shiva mad?"

"Why, what is he to you that you defend him so fiercely?"

"You don't know anything about him. My Lord is far larger than the small and rational mind. Nobody can ever know him. He transcends all virtue and vice. Though he has a body, he is beyond form. Though he is born, he is uncreated and undying. Though he seems far, far away and unattainable, he pulses in my veins and is as close to me as my own heart. And though he seems separate, he and I are one."

"Your words are passionate, but you know nothing of that which you speak. We ascetics are all alike. There is another foolish girl in that village down below this peak who has been pestering me to marry her. Who wants the conflict and battle of being a householder? What women want is the exact opposite of what we yogis want. Take you, for example. You probably want to have babies, do you not?"

"Of course I do. Why shouldn't I want sweet little creatures to suckle and hold and play with? I won't tell Shiva when he comes, but after we are married . . ."

"All women are deceitful. And all they want is trinkets and baubles. You, too, love ornaments, don't you, even though now you are dressed in bark and rags?"

"I dress like this only to please Shiva. He wants me to be a yogini to his yogi, to learn the lesson that in death lies new life, and in denial, renewal. But if you ask me what I truly love, it is life, life, life. I love 'trinkets and baubles,' as you call them. I love to look at rings on my fingers, bracelets on my arms, beautiful stones, precious gems that Nature has perfected in her womb."

"O woman. This body that you pamper and love, whose appetites you do anything to satisfy—it is but ash in the crematoria. If you are buried, maggots will eat it. Why indulge it? Why want palaces and homes for this shell of a thing? You want a home, no?"

"Oh yes, oh yes I do. I love homes, especially fine ones. A kitchen with shining utensils and good food. Comfortable beds covered in clean, silken sheets that do not remain clean for long . . ."

Suddenly Parvati's heart plummeted. Her desire would remain unfulfilled. The beggar was right. Shiva, for whom she longed with a longing like death, would not come for her. "What's the use of these illusions of mine?" she said to the beggar, turning from him in weariness and defeat.

As she began to walk away, the beggar caught hold of her garment. "If you leave me, where will you go? And where can I go without you? You are me, Parvati, and I am you. We are one."

Parvati turned back towards the man, and there, as bright as a thousand suns, was Shiva, the crescent moon shining in his hair, the scales of the cobra around his neck shimmering, his third eye mercifully shut.

Shiva looked deeply into Parvati's eyes, and took her hand. "Come, beloved. Let us dance together, and stir up the universe with mighty churn and pestle."

From all directions of the sky, celestial musicians struck invisible instruments and made divine harmony; heavenly angels appeared from nowhere to dance and rejoice at the cosmic joining together of this long separated couple; flowers rained from the sky as all the gods in heaven looked down upon them and blessed their reunion. Even Shiva's companions, the ghouls from the burning grounds, danced in joy.

As Shiva and Parvati thumped their feet on the mountain side, their eyes locking in love, their limbs moving in dramatic, rhythmic, mythic movements, the universe quaked with delight, the earth shuddered in pleasure, and all the ripe fruit fell off the trees and seeded the earth again.

How Ganesha Got His Elephant Head

Lord Ganesha, elephant-headed god who combines the best of animal and man, fulfiller of earthly desires, patron deity of writers and thieves, beneficent demon who creates obstacles and removes them—omniscient, omnipotent, omnivorous, omnipresent, infinite, boundless, and incomprehensible—was born from the skin cells of his mother, Parvati.

It happened like this:

Parvati and Shiva's marriage settled into a state of alternating bliss and turbulence, both generated by their intense sexuality. As so often happens, the passion of their courtship had temporarily obscured their contrary natures. When Brahma forced them to divide the original essence of their being into its constituent parts, they became positive and negative, Shiva and Shakti. The latter in her incarnations, and especially as Parvati, had more physical mass, and therefore gravitated more towards the concrete: matter, possessions, a house, fine linen, food, sensual delights, and comforts. Shiva, on the contrary, tended towards abstract principles and ideas. Parvati inclined towards the body, and Shiva, the mind; she loved life, and he, death and the company of phantoms and wraiths.

So it was that while Shiva, in his passion for the investigation of consciousness, transcended the biologic imperatives, Shakti, in her manifestation as Parvati, wanted to fulfill her procreative urges. Lately, most of their quarrels had arisen from this root issue. Their opposite natures made their union a blessed return to the state of original beatitude and oneness. But ironically, their ecstatic lovemaking was due to Shiva's control over his ejaculate. He wanted to keep his seed to enhance his spiritual powers, while she wanted it to conceive a child. And this, Shiva was adamantly against.

"Why," he would ask repeatedly, "do you want to bring another being into this grim world that is destined for death, destruction, and decay?"

"No, my Lord, it is destined for life, generation, and joy."

"It is built upon bones and ash, Beloved, which . . ."

". . . are fodder for flowers, trees, animals, people, and babies!"

"Our task here is awareness, the conquering of our lower natures, and . . ."

"No, no, my Lord, everywhere in nature, of which we are part, we see generative powers at work. Our task is to perpetuate consciousness. In four billion and eight thousand million years we will be dead, and then who will . . ."

"Let others take care of that. The world is full of people who are rutting to engender offspring, but this lifetime I want to devote to . . ."

"Don't I matter? Don't you care about my needs? My body is aching for a child. I am deeply unhappy at your . . ."

Whenever the quarrel began to spiral down to a fight, Shiva simply got off the bed, and walked out of the house.

This dialogue in its permutations repeated itself consistently, over and over, for a thousand or so years. Parvati, her fertility waning with years, was nearing the end of her patience. When dialogue, sweetness, anger, rage, and guile failed, she tried to woo him with poetry, song, and her vast repertoire of feminine charms, but Shiva remained unyielding, like stone. The more she asked, begged, and pleaded, the more immovable he became. Their battles always ended in separation. Shiva left to meditate in remote and inaccessible regions of India, and Parvati settled into her solitude in their small house provided for her by her father, Himavat, Lord of the Himalayas.

While Shiva slept in graveyards and cremations grounds, with ash for his bed, Parvati had some measure of comfort and luxury in her home. With all the riches from Himavat's domains—gold from the veins of mountains, quartz, rubies, lapis, amethyst, rare herbs and spices, lumber and stone—Parvati lacked nothing. One of her delights was a warm bath in a huge abalone shell unearthed from the ground.

It had lain there from the time—a blink and a half ago of Brahma's eyes—when the folds of the Himalayas formed the ocean floor. She would fill the shell with water from hot springs, dissolve unguents and perfumes in it, smear herself with pastes of sandalwood, turmeric, and exotic fruits, and take long baths.

One day, as she finished her bath and was rubbing herself down with oil, she saw the skin slough in the cup of her hand. An idea entered her head, and she laughed so loudly that in a violent outburst galaxies collided in the firmament and birthed stars in luminescent clouds of whirling, iridescent gas.

"I don't need Shiva's seed to reproduce!" Parvati realized in an outburst of pride. "I have the wherewithal for it myself! The tissues and cells from my scurf contain all the material to make a child."

Parvati knew she had the power. She was a manifestation of the creative energy of the universe, the very matrix from which all life comes. Being a goddess, she could look into the structure of a cell and see what a wonderful mechanism it was! It could move, breathe, digest, eliminate, and reproduce itself.

"How glorious is the body," she thought, bursting into a paean. "How miraculous this flesh and blood, these organs, membranes, cartilage and bone. And all of it is alive and pulsing with mystery. Life, potent life, can be created out of every cell of my body. Oh what a marvelous machine this is!"

There were some matters in which Parvati had to beat out her own path on this planet. Her hunger for reproduction would not be denied or betrayed now, even if it meant a break from Shiva. Separation from him was not new to her. She had spent entire lifetimes alone when Shiva had been as recalcitrant as a mule to her truths and needs. In one of her lifetimes, in another age of Brahma, Shakti had manifested as Kali, the Wronged Woman Turned Warrior, irrepressible, independent, and full of power. She could be alone again if need be.

She placed the flakes of her plasma in the large abalone shell that had held her bathwater and unguents. Standing naked over it, still wet from her bath, she uttered a mantra of desire. Her breath pierced the membrane of one of the cells, and mixing with the microscopic matter in the nucleus, fertilized it.

Parvati became aware of a vibration so soft as to be imperceptible to all but the most trained and passionate of ears. It was as if all matter in the universe was resonating to a low hum, which activated the energy that caused the cell to divide and multiply rapidly. Swelling to the gentle throbbing of the vibration, the single cell became a cluster of cells, the beaded bodies unraveled into the divine double helix, and in the flash of an eye, the fetus became an embryo, going through all its phases. The spine developed, the holy heart began to beat to the sound of dramatic drums, the lungs began to pulse with air, and the entire mass quickened into immortal life.

The low hum swelled into a symphony of celestial music, culminating in a great crashing crescendo of joy and celebration that proclaimed that a great being, trailing stardust and glorious dirt, son of heaven and earth, offspring of sound and silence, body and mind, time and eternity, had made his appearance on the stage of the world.

A cherubic, chubby child with folds of skin upon his belly lay waving his arms and legs in the shell, and laughing delightedly. As he opened his eyes, the light from them brightened the world with sunshine.

He stretched, and his stretching was a dance. Rolling over, he stood on all fours, straightened up, and before Parvati's eyes, misted and sloshing over with rivers of maternal love, he danced his birth dance, turning and whirling about a center in lyrical spirals from which streamed bright specks whirling in streams of light.

Parvati watched in awe at what she had created: this flesh of her own flesh, in slow, measured steps moving in a manner reminiscent of her own dance with Shiva in Tillai, the center of the world. This child was, without the shadow of a doubt, Shiva's son also. The breath that had fertilized her baby boy was Shiva's breath. How could it not be? Through their many separations, they remained indissolubly united, one. This was the child of their inseparable union.

Parvati's pride in having created him herself paused and abated. She breathed deeply, and released from the chains of leaden pride, joined her son in the dance. They wheeled around each other to the music of the spheres in a constellation that included the specter of Shiva. When the dance was done, Parvati named their son Ganesha, Lord of the Celestial Deities.

Ganesha, the child of Parvati's cosmic desire, bringing together the best energies of the universe, was a beautiful, plump boy. He spent his time frolicking, playing the drum, dancing, singing, and eating to his heart's content all the wonderful food that his mother made for him. But having no male role model, he grew up spoiled, vain, proud of his beauty, and of being the son of the most important goddess on earth.

As an adult, Ganesha knew that unless he found a woman equal in beauty and power to his mother, he would remain celibate.

For many years that passed in a blink of time, Parvati played at being a mother and delighted in all the joys of a long-denied motherhood. She didn't miss Shiva, who was off on his own inner journey, worshiping and communing with the dark energies of the universe.

One spring day as Parvati watched the buds on trees swelling and bursting forth into the blue air to the cracking of ice, the lover in her, not fulfilled entirely with just the mothering role, thawed and awoke. Her body aroused, she instinctively thought of Shiva. How long it had been since she had looked into his eyes, and felt his skin next to hers! Her longing bridged the distance between them in one instant. Love dissipated Space-Time, which she knew to be a mere construct of the mind. All her memories of their fighting were as chaff in the wind, and only the grain of their love remained. Parvati knew that when her longing got this intense, Shiva's thoughts and body, too, were turning towards her. "Shiva, Shiva, Shiva," she repeated in her mind, and immediately went into a trance, her eyes weeping rivers of love that sprang from her melted heart.

Certain of his inevitable and imminent return, Parvati prepared her bath with crushed grapes and cream, jasmines and rose petals, pollens and stamens of rare flowers that were beyond naming. She called Ganesha and told him to stand guard outside their house and let no one enter. She wanted to ensure that no one came in while she was bathing. Lately, Kubera, Lord of Gold, who had always had a keen eye for Parvati in his mistaken hope that she might turn to him in her loneliness during Shiva's long absences, had taken to visiting at all hours.

"Fool," she thought. "As if anything can lure me away from my Shiva."

Parvati's other reason for posting Ganesha was a clever and ill-advised one. Ganesha was a really good-looking youth, and Shiva had never seen him before nor knew who he was. Would Shiva be jealous? Would his passion for her be doubly aroused?

If Parvati had known then the terrible consequences of her cleverness, she would probably still have done what she did. Destiny has a way of fulfilling itself through mistakes and perversities. In this case, Ganesha was meant to be greater and far more extraordinary than he was, and his own ego and Parvati's cleverness became the means for it.

While standing guard outside his mother's bath, Ganesha saw a travel-worn, dust- and ash-covered, naked beggar with a snake around his neck approaching, and prepared to defend his home with the mace in his hand. Shiva saw a handsome youth guarding his home, and his suspicions were immediately aroused. He was further incensed when Ganesha denied him entry into his own home.

"Whoever you are, you can't enter," Ganesha said. "Goddess Parvati is in her bath."

"Don't you know who I am?" Shiva thundered. "I am Parvati's husband."

Ganesha laughed aloud derisively.

"Parvati's husband! You? Parvati's husband? Find some other delusion, mendicant. This one is going to get you beaten to a pulp," Ganesha said, waving his mace in the air.

"Who on earth are you?" Shiva said, tightening his hold on his trident.

"Where have you been? Everyone knows who I am. I am the marvelous goddess's splendid . . . son," Ganesha said.

Shiva let the implication sink in. Rage arose in him like a thunderstorm at the thought of his wife with another man. Had she finally succumbed to the seductions of that slimy Lord of Gold, Kubera? Suddenly Shiva was not the Lord of Songs, Divine Physician, the Blue-Throated, Tranquil God of Ascetics, the Sweet-Scented Lover of Parvati, but the Terrible and Fierce Lord of Destruction. In one quick and powerful movement, he swung his trident, and decapitated the youth.

The commotion outside and Ganesha's scream brought Parvati out of her house, confusion crowding into her soul. Her ecstasy at seeing her husband was balanced with the agony at the sight of her son's decapitated body. She laughed and wept, ranted, raved, and in a rush related the entire story of Ganesha's birth to Shiva.

"He is my son, he is our son, Shiva! The breath that fertilized him was yours! His dance—which you will never see now unless you repair the damage you have done—is your dance, our dance!"

Shiva was stricken with remorse at the sight of Parvati beating her breasts and wailing. Spring receded and all around them the budding trees became bare rods again, the blue skies turned dark and thunderous, and in no time, snow covered the mountainside and the river turned again to ice.

Shiva turned and left to see if he could find either a head to replace the one he had struck off, or a body to fit the head. He roamed far and wide in an instant, without success. In a forest he heard a trumpeting sound, and there before him stood the demon elephant, Gajasura, his trunk in the air, his small, dark eyes rolling, his feet stomping the earth rhythmically and powerfully.

Now, Gajasura, even though he was an evil demon, was a great devotee of Shiva's. Before and after every evil deed, he danced and sang to Shiva; at awaking and before sleeping, he prayed to Shiva; before setting out in search of food, before stomping to death any animal, before capturing a bird and crushing it to death with his strong, muscular trunk, he would dedicate his acts to Shiva.

Shiva was most pleased to come upon Gajasura in his travels. Gajasura knelt down and bowed to Shiva with such gentleness and humility, that Shiva said instinctively,

"Ask, Gajasura, and I will grant you a wish!"

"Lord," said Gajasura, looking at Shiva with devotion and love, "I have waited my whole life for just this moment. I never again want to be parted from you. I pray you, let me eat you, so I will always have you within me."

"Granted," said Shiva. Ecstatic that his wish had been granted, Gajasura tenderly wrapped his trunk around Shiva, carried him to his mouth, and swallowed him.

A tremor was felt in Heaven, and Vishnu and Brahma knew immediately what had happened. Disguised as a musician and his drummer, Vishnu and Brahma arrived at the spot on earth where Gajasura sat on his haunches, unbelievably content with his divine meal. He had achieved his life's goal, and was certain that he would never more be parted from his god. And now, as if to crown his joy and celebrate his victory, came the best musicians he had ever heard.

He relaxed further, enjoying his after dinner entertainment thoroughly. When Vishnu and Brahma were done, Gajasura said magnanimously,

"Ask, divine musicians, for a boon, and you shall be granted your wish."

"Lord Gajasura, we ask that you return our Shiva to us."

Tears began to course down Gajasura's rough cheeks. He knew that in granting the musicians' wish, he had decreed his own end. Together with this realization came total surrender of his life and body to the gods before him. The presence of Shiva in his belly made him calm, even joyous, at his approaching death. It was enough for him to have had Shiva in his stomach for just an instant. It had enlightened him, dissolved all his evil tendencies, and made him divine.

"Even though you take Shiva away from me, you cannot part me from Shiva ever again," Gajasura said. "We have become one in substance and in spirit." Gajasura raised his trunk, opened his mouth, and disgorged Shiva.

In his death throes, Gajasura said, "Lord, take my head which has schemed and devised for centuries. I bequeath it to you. Take this head, now cleansed of its cleverness, its egotistical self-will and arrogance, and make it immortal. Make it so that everyone will worship it. Take it now, while I still live. I surrender it to your purposes."

Vishnu, Brahma, and Shiva severed the demon's head, chanting and singing all the while. In an instant that took no time, all three of them arrived where Ganesha lay torn in two, and Shiva, the divine physician, transplanted the elephant head to his son's body.

While Parvati wondered if the head was too large, Shiva looked at his son with pride and joy, Vishnu with wonder, and Brahma with awe at the sight before them—Ganesha, elephant-headed, majestic, powerful, absurd, comical, dramatic, adorable, lovable, worshipable, all rolled into one. And before their eyes, Ganesha's girth swelled in proportion to his head, and became the girth of the bountiful earth, containing the world in its rotundity.

Brahma struck his drums, Vishnu broke into song, and Shiva began to dance. And oh, what a dance it was! His son, transformed, newly resurrected, joined him and began to dance, too. If Parvati had any doubt about the proportions of her son, they dissolved at the sight before her. Ganesha was more stupendous than he had ever been, his footsteps lighter and more lyrical now that he had gained the instinctive grace of animals. And so happy was she at being reunited with her son and her husband as Vishnu and Brahma themselves provided the accompaniment to the festivities, that Parvati, too, began to dance.

And if Shiva had any doubts about Ganesha's paternity, they vanished at the sight of his son's dance, which equaled his own in its beauty and magic. Shiva knew that in time he, Lord of Detachment, would also live in domestic bliss for brief spells, and delight in the joys of a family.

Swaying and swinging, Ganesha wrapped his trunk lovingly around his parents, and hoisted them into the air as the entire heavenly host rejoiced at the reunion of this celestial family.

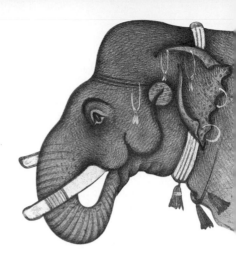

GANESHA GOES TO LUNCH

Kubera, who lived in the city of Alkapuri, was the king of the Yakshasas, creatures who were born hungry, needy, and greedy. As soon as they came into the world, they began to devour everything. Their first and only words were, "Eat! Eat! Eat." Nor did their ravenous consumption confine itself to ordinary, edible fare. They ate entire mountains and vast chunks of the earth to extract gold, diamonds, and gems, hoarding and eating them at will. Never satisfied, they took to eating entire trees, forests, rivers, boulders, houses, storehouses full of grains and fruit, and even human beings.

Kubera, because he was a ruthless and indiscriminate eater, soon earned the title King of Gold. He was the wealthiest man of the world and had everything that humans could possibly desire of material goods: many huge palaces replete with the richest and finest of furnishings; treasuries full of gold and jewels; all manner of food, chariots, servants, and maids; useful and fanciful gadgets from all over the world, as well as all the amusements a greedy man could imagine. He possessed the coveted Pushpaka, the greatest of vehicles. It utilized the ash of three burned forests to run for just a second. Mind-propelled, it rose into the air at the owner's will, soaring above the other traffic of the crowded city, and traversed huge distances in the shortest amount of time. It could also expand according to need, and assume the proportions of a huge city. Kubera would host parties in it and invite all the people of power and beauty to travel and feast in it. One of his greatest pleasures was to fly it slowly in the air, just so people, on seeing its shadow, would crane their necks, wonder at it, and be consumed by envy.

But no matter how much Kubera had, there always remained something else that he had to have. He became obsessed with the craving to possess the goddess Parvati. The goddess would be his crown jewel, and make him the envy of every man on earth.

He was certain that he could win her. Undeterred by the fact that Parvati and Shiva had turned down a thousand of his invitations to lunch, he kept his hope alive—convinced that gold was the only way to a woman's heart. One day Parvati was going to accept his invitation, and then she would be his. How could she resist the temptation of such wealth? All women need comforts, riches, and servants. If only Parvati would dine at his palace, Kubera would show her what she was missing with that matt-haired mendicant Shiva, who couldn't even provide Parvati with a home! No wonder they fought so much. Everyone had heard of their quarrels. When Shiva and Parvati fought, the earth swung on its axis and the world wobbled madly. But with Kubera, the King of Gold, she would fulfill her heart's desires and be content.

Once more, he penned an invitation with letters of gold upon the best of parchments, and donned his finest clothes and jewels. He would take the invitation to Shiva and Parvati's humble home himself—riding in Pushpaka! Even if Parvati refused the invitation to lunch again, she was sure to at least glimpse his vehicle, and want it!

In their home, Parvati and Shiva had just finished making love and were lying in each other's arms, talking and laughing, when they heard the beautiful, though loud music that Pushpaka made while landing.

"It is that fool, Kubera," Parvati said, turning her head towards the window. "He thinks he can seduce me with his toys."

"Can't he?" Shiva asked, twisting a lock of her hair in his fingers. "Everyone knows you're always fighting with me because you want this or that."

"But I want them from you, my Shiva, nobody else. Only you."

"You have fought with me many times over wanting this or that. What women want is . . ."

". . . love before all else, my Lord. Love alone satisfies all hungers."

Shiva pulled Parvati to him, and kissed her. "Kubera has undoubtedly come with another invitation. Shall we accept this one?" Shiva asked.

"No, let's send Ganesha. He has been looking thin lately, and needs a good meal," laughed Parvati. Parvati got off the bed, opened the door a crack and said to Ganesha, "Accept his invitation and go to lunch with the King of Gold, Ganesha. And enjoy yourself!" Then she returned to the bed, nestled close to Shiva, and began to recall stories about Ganesha.

"Remember that time when we went for a picnic to the shores of the Milky Way? Ganesha thought it was milk, stuck his trunk into the ocean of stars, and sucked it all up."

"Including Vishnu, Lakshmi, Shesh Nag, Brahma, and Indra!"

"The world would have come to an end if Ganesha hadn't burped after his meal! And they all came tumbling out!"

"Remember the time . . ."

Kubera leaped off Pushpaka, and came to the door, all his jewels flashing in the sun. He was met at the door by Ganesha. Kubera felt disappointment tug at his heart, but cheered himself with the thought that his meeting Ganesha was a good sign. This time there would be no obstacles to his desire. And sure enough, his heart somersaulted madly at Ganesha's next words:

"Your invitation has been accepted!"

Kubera beamed at him. Parvati was already his!

"By me!" said Ganesha.

It took Kubera a minute to realize what had happened. Not Parvati, but Ganesha was coming to lunch. He was beginning to feel crushed when he consoled himself with the thought that Ganesha was sure to return home and tell his mother about all the wonders that he had seen.

He took Ganesha aboard his vessel, and took him to the most opulent of his palaces in Alkapuri. As soon as they landed, Kubera wanted to give him a tour of his mansion and treasury, but Ganesha was very hungry and wanted to eat first.

Ganesha sat down at the table set with gold plates and cutlery studded with diamonds and gems, and Kubera sat down proudly beside him. Ganesha was impressed. The gold serving bowls contained delicious-looking dainties, the like of which Ganesha had neither seen nor tasted before. Kubera's chefs from all over the world had prepared them with the rarest of ingredients, herbs, spices, and condiments. Servants put generous helpings of each of the many dishes on Ganesha's golden plate, and he ate heartily, chewing slowly and savoring every mouthful. Never, not even in the heavenly kitchen of his mother, Parvati, had he tasted anything like this.

Ganesha asked for more, and Kubera, pleased that the cuisine's excellence had aroused his guest's appetite, motioned to the servants to heap food high upon Ganesha's plate again. This time Ganesha ate the food very quickly, shoveling delicacies into his mouth with his trunk. When the plate was clean, he asked for more, and was given it. Ganesha found that the more he ate of Kubera's food, the more ravenous he became. So, when the long row of servers brought the salvers and dishes in, Ganesha wrapped his trunk around each of the dishes and emptied them into his mouth. Again and again he was served, and again and again he asked for more and more till the food was all gone.

"More!" cried Ganesha. The serving men looked at Kubera and shook their heads to say that no more food remained. Kubera asked them to bring in the dessert. Ganesha consumed every wonderful sweet dish brought to him. He no longer made pretence of taking small help-

ings, but grasped serving bowls with his trunk, and instead of emptying them into his mouth, put the entire gold serving dish into his mouth and munched it all up.

"More!" cried Ganesha. "It's not enough!"

"Sire," the cooks said, wringing their hands. "There isn't any left!"

But by now Ganesha's hunger had been aroused to such a pitch that he had to eat more, and eat whatever he could. He ate up the entire cutlery with a crunching sound. Kubera, whose amazement had grown to an astounding degree, just sat there and stared at his guest with bewilderment in his eyes.

Ganesha's stomach had become an empty pit that expanded with each morsel he put into it. Irrational and crazy with an appetite that had begun to consume him instead, Ganesha rushed into the kitchen and ate all the utensils one by one, while the cooks looked on with eyes wide with disbelief and relief. They wouldn't have to do the dishes after this feast. This was the most unusual dinner they had cooked and served. This was almost—if it weren't also a bit scary—fun. And when Ganesha had cleaned up the kitchen, he returned to the dining room and began swallowing up the chairs and table.

The servants, who had followed Ganesha back to the dining room, marveled at the spectacle before them, certain that the furniture would be the last thing he ate. Surely these huge helpings would glut his appetite. But the elephant god had not had enough, and demanded more again.

To distract his guest, Kubera took Ganesha to his treasury to show off all his coins, ingots of gold and glorious jewelry. But no sooner did Ganesha enter than Kubera knew it was a terrible mistake. Ganesha emptied the trunks of gold, one after the other, into his mouth, till not an ounce of gold remained—then began to gnaw on the jewels and jewelry. But even these satisfied Ganesha not a jot, but aroused his omnivorous appetite even further.

Kubera looked on speechlessly. He was too polite to refuse anything to a guest of Ganesha's stature, yet realized he was being literally eaten out of hearth and home. And despite this, Ganesha looked at him and said, simply "This isn't enough."

"But I don't know what else I can serve you," Kubera said, just before he caught sight of a glint in Ganesha's eyes that made the host turn and run down the hall and out the door.

"I must get to Shiva and Parvati and ask them to rescue me from their monster son," Kubera thought as he rushed to Pushpaka, climbed aboard, and took off. But Ganesha had coiled his trunk around one of its wheels and accompanied Kubera all the way back to his parents' house.

Kubera landed outside Shiva and Parvati's home, and ran into the house. Ganesha, however, looked at Pushpaka as if it were a delightful tidbit, and gulped it down in one swallow!

"Oh no, not my magic transport!" cried Kubera, looking back at the sight of his precious possession flying down Ganesha's gullet. He flung open the door and rushed into the house, shrieking, "Help me! Help me! Lord Shiva! Goddess Parvati! Help me! Save me from your son!"

Shiva and Parvati, sitting side by side, looked at each other, and smiled. "What's the matter?" Parvati asked Kubera innocently.

"He has eaten up everything I own! And now he wants to eat me! O, help me, save me from him, my Lord and Lady!" Kubera threw himself at their feet, clasping them in his hands.

Kubera had only meant to ask them for their help, but was amazed how contact with their feet flooded him with insights about the cause of his misfortunes: his greed, pride, and vanity had brought him to this point. Ganesha had merely held up a mirror and reflected his own face back at him.

Kubera heard a trumpeting sound, and there stood Ganesha in the doorway, his eyes rolling in a hungry frenzy, heading his way. Ganesha's appetite was still unabated, and he wanted to see if devouring Kubera, God of Gold, would sate it.

Parvati entered her kitchen and returned hurriedly, handing Kubera a small, earthenware bowl of rice pudding that she had made lovingly with her own hands. "Here," she said. "Feed him this with love, Lord Kubera, and he will calm down."

Kubera looked at Ganesha, as if for the first time, and all at once love and adoration arose in his heart for this being that had stripped him of all his wealth—but bestowed upon him the invaluable gift of vision. He went up to Ganesha, and with his own hand, fed him a handful of the pudding.

No sooner had the pudding touched the buds of his mouth than Ganesha calmed down and lost the unfocused and whirling glint in his eyes. He walked meekly to his mother and coiled his trunk playfully around her.

"Go home, Lord Kubera," Parvati said, "and you will find all your wealth restored to you. The material world and its comforts exist for our delight, but you cannot destroy society and mother earth to get them. Learn what enough is, and remember that true wealth can only be built on the foundation of humility and love."

"And learn to discriminate between legitimate desires and cravings," Shiva added, putting his arm around Parvati while Ganesha wrapped his trunk lovingly around his body.

Kubera bowed and retreated. Ganesha settled down at his parents' feet and fell asleep instantly after his rather huge meal.

A Story of
Krishna and
Some Parables

Introduction to a Story of Krishna and Some Parables

Krishna is one of Vishnu's ten incarnations, which begin with lower life forms, like fish, tortoise, boar, and end in the gods, Lord Rama (hero of the epic, the Ramayana), Lord Krishna, and Lord Buddha. For many Hindus this progression is analogous to Darwin's theory of evolution.

Krishna holds the honor of being one of India's favorite gods, hence there are many legends and fables about him in the different stages of his life.

As a divine child Krishna is full of pranks, mischief and miracles: he steals butter from the kitchens of housewives, breaks their clay pots full of milk and yogurt, and with butter still clinging to his lips and cheeks, blatantly denies eating it. Stealing the garments of young women bathing in the river, he climbs a tree, and refuses to return the clothes till they come to him naked and shivering.

As a youth Krishna is the object of erotic love for girls, women, boys, men, sages, saints and holy men, who hearken to the sound of his flute, and abandon their ordinary lives to follow its call to spiritual adventure.

As an adult Krishna embodies the source of all wisdom, which he imparts to Arjuna on the battle field, and which comprises one of India's holiest texts, the *Bhagawad Gita*, translated variously as the Song of the Divine One, the Song of God, or the Song of Love.

In it Krishna, represented as the Supreme Being, gives Arjuna spiritual guidance that has continued to inspire and instruct human kind through the centuries.

Sudama is Krishna's beloved childhood friend. A poor person and a commoner, he represents "everyman." Sudama makes frequent appearances in legends in oral tradition that sprang up round Krishna. Perhaps the meaning of this popular story featuring Sudama is that Krishna, the Ocean of Love, loves all. He is especially fond of those who long for him, the way Sudama does.

The rest of the characters in this section need no introduction, as they are people and animals in obscure parables invented by holy men for our instruction and amusement.

THE MILLION STEPS

Krishna and Sudama were childhood friends. They played in the forests of Vrindavana, pilfered butter from the larders of housewives, herded cows, and stole the clothes of the women and girls bathing in the Jamuna River. But the best of their times were when they made music together. While Krishna played his flute, Sudama accompanied him on his ek tara, a one-stringed gourd which he sometimes plucked with his fingers, and sometimes plied with a bow.

They grew up and their ways parted; Krishna moved to Dwarka, they lost touch with each other, and years passed.

Sudama came from a poor family and inherited his father's poverty. He married, had children, tilled and ploughed someone else's fields, and herded other people's cows so he could afford just enough provisions to feed his wife and children. There were never any new clothes, and the old ones were patched and falling apart; their house was not safe against the wind, or cold, or rain.

Through all of it, Sudama's one consolation was his musical gourd. He would keep it in tune, and would compose and play songs on it on days when he had a little respite from labor, but mainly in the dead of night, his longing for Krishna swelling and dilating his heart. The ek tara connected him to Krishna right away, bringing the holy one near, as close as his heart. But whenever Sudama didn't play it—which was most of the time, because of too much work, too many mouths to feed, and too many people to placate and please—he was like a fish out of water, gasping for air. His lungs would slacken, sleep would flee, and his body would drag about from chore to chore, as if he were half-dead.

Often, he would dream that Krishna was calling to him with his flute. Sudama would arise from his bed like a swan, and fly to meet Krishna on his wide, white wings. But Sudama always awoke in his bed in his shack, with no sign of Krishna whatsoever. His dream always left him disturbed, so disturbed that he could find relief only in doubt. It was a dream, he would tell himself again and again, a crazy, silly, childish dream. There was nothing true about it at all. He had to behave and live like other men, and take care of all those responsibilities that were the lot of the earthbound human animal.

But being a singer and a musician by temperament complicated his life terribly. He spent half his life having dreams and visions of Krishna, who he adored, and the other half doubting them. The combination of his practical and visionary life caused him to lead a secret double life. The axis of one of them was Krishna, and the focus of the other was doubt. The further he moved from his childhood, the more the latter grew. And the more it grew, the crazier Sudama became.

During one such time, when Sudama was particularly numb and lifeless, his wife, Padmini, said to him, "Jee, I have been thinking, why don't you visit Krishna?" Sudama grew very silent and still at his secret name thus being spoken aloud by another. "I have heard that he is a big lord now, very wealthy. Some even call him the Lord of the Universe. Perhaps he could help us," she said.

Sudama's heart fluttered at the thought of meeting Krishna again. A warmth suffused his heart and hope stirred in his breast. But immediately on the heels of that thought came despair: what had he to show for his life? Surely Krishna had forgotten all about him. Why would such an important man bother with the likes of him? No, it was pointless and impossible. He would not go.

"If your childhood love was true, Jee, Krishna will care for you still. Remember that bhajan you used to sing?" Padmini said, and began to hum:

> *If you take one step towards God,*
> *God will take a million towards you.*

Sudama was thrilled to hear the singing voice of his wife again. He hadn't heard it for so many years! Before the children came, they would often sit and sing together. Padmini, too, was surprised by how good it

felt to sing!

"You'll go, won't you?"

"No," said Sudama. "I don't want to be humiliated."

But Padmini did not give up on the idea. She kept bringing it up, eroding his resistance. One morning, after another of his dreams in which he thought he heard, vaguely, the sound of Krishna's flute, Sudama decided to go to Dwarka. With holes in his shoes, a shirt so faded and worn that he wondered if it would last him till his destination, and his little gourd, Sudama prepared for his journey with a mixture of hope and doubt, excitement and trepidation in his heart.

"Here," said Padmini, handing him a small and dirty-looking pouch in which she had wrapped some rice puffs with roasted kernels of corn. "Give this to him when you meet him. One must not go empty-handed to meet an old friend. And remember to ask him to help us."

Sudama set out on his journey to meet Krishna. The little treat in his pocket brought back memories of when they would play together in the forests, climb trees, sit astride the branches, watch the girls bathing, and munch on puffed wheat or corn kernels. How Krishna would eat them, rolling them first in the cupped palm of his hand, then tossing them into his mouth! How delicious they had tasted after a day of vigorous playing!

What a time that was! How carefree and innocent! How little it mattered that he, Sudama, was poor, and that Krishna's foster parents were rich. How dearly they loved each other, and how deeply attached Sudama had been to him. There was not a day they didn't meet, and not a night when the thought of his friend did not warm his heart with a bright glow.

And then everything changed that day when Krishna's foster mother, Yashoda, caught them eating clay from the riverbed.

"Did you eat clay?" Yashoda scolded Krishna.

"No," replied Krishna, innocently.

"Open your mouth and let me see!" Krishna opened his mouth and both Yashoda and Sudama had stepped back in awe and wonder at what they saw in Krishna's mouth: the swirling globe of the blue green earth oscillating upon its axis, and revolving with its moon and other planets around the sun!

For days Sudama had walked around stunned, unable to comprehend what he had seen, feeling half-mad, ecstatic, alive, levitating above the earth, disturbed, and afraid, terribly afraid that a being such as

Krishna was far beyond his own status and reach. He had felt miniscule in comparison, a mere human, and had withdrawn in his heart.

When Sudama reached Dwarka, he did not need to find out where Krishna lived, for all roads in Dwarka led to his palace. He could see its columns and turrets from a distance, all lit up and sparkling. His heart sinking with doubt, Sudama sat beneath a tree, wondering whether he should turn back to Vrindavana. What was the point? Krishna would not remember him. Or, even if there was the slightest chance that Krishna might, how could Sudama, dirty and ragged, be permitted into his presence? The guards would see to it that he didn't even get close. Yes, it might be best to turn back now.

But Sudama was tired after his long journey, and decided to rest before starting back. He worried about what he would tell Padmini. How disappointed she would be, for she had placed a great deal of hope in this meeting.

He lay down under a tree, his heart heavy and hopeless within him, and fell into a deep and leaden slumber. He dreamt about a day long ago when, on the banks of the Jamuna, Krishna had plunged into the river to do battle with the terrible serpent, Kaliya, who was devastating the village, swallowing the cattle, and keeping the girls from bathing. Krishna climbed a tree above the river and dove in. The splash roiled the waters and awoke Kaliya, slumbering in the depths after a heavy meal of two cows and a goat. The creature's huge body undulated towards Krishna, hood fanned, fangs ready to inject their poison into the intruder. And though Krishna struggled against him, Kaliya was very powerful, and overcame him.

Sudama peered through the clear waters and saw Kaliya's muscular length wrapped tightly around Krishna's feet, legs, torso, neck, face, and head, biting Krishna over and over and pumping venom into his veins. And Krishna lay there limp, lifeless, and inert. Sudama's heart sank into utter despair. He had lost his friend forever! And along with all the villagers who stood and watched, he began to moan and weep.

But Balarama, Krishna's brother, spoke to Krishna from the banks and said, "Lord of the Universe, remember who you are! Don't allow your mortality to cloud your essence and your strength! Shake off this seeming weakness, these illusions of fetters. Arise and conquer this demon!"

And behold, Krishna opened one eye wide, smiled, and with one mighty heave of his arms shook himself free. He leaped upon the serpent's head, and began to dance upon it!

As he slept, it seemed to Sudama that Krishna was now dancing upon his heart as if it were a drum, arousing it with the beat of his sacred feet.

Sudama awoke with a start, and sat up under the tree. The dream was a message from Krishna! "If I can free myself thus from the grasp of the dreadful Kaliya, you can free yourself from the crippling coils of doubt. Arise and dance upon the head of your despair, Sudama!"

This vision gave Sudama the courage to dare to venture towards Krishna's palace. Placing the neck of the gourd on his shoulder beneath his chin, and plying the bow with his other hand, he set out to meet Krishna. He would focus just on the sound of his music, and imagine that Krishna could hear it.

Miraculously, no guards were present; the gates of the palace stood wide open as Sudama approached them and entered. Inside, however, he was stricken again with his own smallness and insignificance. A thousand accomplished musicians and minstrels with various instruments, unique rhythms, and exquisite voices were all singing the praises of Krishna in one magnificent harmony: wind, water, fire, and all the minor and major gods— Indra, Brahma, Shiva, Devis, Devatas—all sang with their splendid voices of his power and magnificence, while all the planets, the sun, the moon, and the stars danced around him to the music. The sound of Sudama's ek tara was quite lost in it.

How pitiful his own little music seemed to him! How worthless his little gift of rice puffs! He wished he could instantly disappear and find himself back in his home in Vrindavana.

In the midst of the chorus of sounds, Sudama heard, distant at first, but getting closer, the sound of Krishna's flute. He closed his eyes to listen. Then slowly it came near, very near, as near as his own heartbeat. And then the ragged visitor heard a familiar voice call him by his name: "Sudama!" And then again, "Sudama!"

As Sudama opened his eyes, before him stood Krishna himself, flute in hand, a smile on his lips. Was it just another dream? Disbelieving his own eyes, he watched as Krishna lifted his arms and placed them on Sudama's shoulders. "Now surely he will turn away from me," Sudama thought.

"I'm sorry . . . " began Sudama, but knew suddenly that he had no need to be. Krishna was not looking at his clothes or shoes, but directly into his heart. Sudama looked back into Krishna's eyes, feeling the ecstatic flow of a river emptying into an ocean. Krishna pulled Sudama to him and embraced him, holding him close. "You didn't summon me, and I longed and longed for you," sobbed Sudama on Krishna's shoulder.

"Dear, dear friend, I called you every night, but your doubting mind stood in your way. How long I have waited for you to come!" Krishna said, wiping Sudama's tears. "Come, let us play together."

Sudama tucked the gourd beneath his chin again, and began to play to the melody of Krishna's flute. Around them, the host of devotees and dancers vanished. There was only Krishna and Sudama, playing together again as in their childhood, as in Sudama's dreams. As they did, Krishna's palace disappeared; even Sudama's body disappeared. Nothing remained save the pure and disembodied resonance of their love.

"I'm hungry," Krishna said. "Where are my rice puffs?" Sudama opened his eyes and saw Krishna's outstretched hand.

With hesitance, Sudama brought out the pouch Padmini had given him: "What an insignificant gift to bring for the Lord of the Universe," he thought. But Krishna took it eagerly, opened it, and tossed handfuls into his mouth, just as he had done when they were children.

Taking a kernel from his mouth, Krishna tossed it into the air. Before Sudama's eyes the kernel swirled and swelled into the globe of the earth, oscillating in space. Krishna grabbed the kernel with his hand and placed it in Sudama's mouth. And all Sudama's doubts about himself and Krishna dissolved like a mountain of smoke.

Sudama stayed at Dwarka for many days, as if in a trance, playing and listening to music, and being near Krishna. Soon it was time for him to leave, and Sudama felt great sorrow. "Know that I am as near you as your heart, Sudama. We shall never more be parted." As Krishna spoke, Sudama felt this truth reverberating through every cell of his body.

At peace now, Sudama set out for Vrindavana again. On the road back he found a small shack abandoned by a hermit, and rested in it. A small stream strewn with boulders flowed there, and hot springs bubbled up from deep within the earth. Here he played his music and sang his songs as an accompaniment to Krishna's unheard, though everywhere present, flute. A great bliss vibrated in his heart in which Krishna dwelt constantly now.

Sudama was halfway home before he remembered that he hadn't asked Krishna to help his family. So content had he been in his company, that Sudama had forgotten all lack. "What shall I tell Padmini?"

he thought. "She will certainly be angry with me."

Weeks later, he arrived in Vrindavana. At the site where his shack had been, stood a stone and wood bungalow, surrounded by a fine garden. For an instant Sudama grew agitated. What had happened in his absence? Where were his wife and children? Did something terrible happen to them while he was away? But when the door opened, there stood Padmini and his sons, no longer in torn and tattered clothes, but well attired, looking healthy and pleased.

"Oh, Jee," his wife said joyfully, "I told you, did I not, that if you take one step towards God, he takes a million towards you?"

Padmini proudly showed Sudama around the house. It was beautiful and spacious, furnished with rich bedspreads and carpets. There were servants and maids, chariots and charioteers, gold and jewels in the trunk, and food aplenty in the kitchen.

"Oh, my wife! I don't want any of this," Sudama said. "I want to live in the small hut I found on my way back from Dwarka. I want to live simply, meditate, and merge the meager sound of my ek tara and my voice to the great symphony of Krishna's praise, and devote my life to him who has given us everything we have. Krishna is our true wealth, beloved. Let us leave these riches for our sons, and go there."

"Please, Jee!" pleaded Padmini. "Just one year in luxury! I am very tired from all these years of working, cooking, cleaning, washing and mending clothes, collecting firewood, hunting for food in field and forest, and making peace between our children. Please let me have just a year of rest and relaxation."

Sudama consented, knowing that when you are anchored in Krishna, a year is just half a blink of time. Padmini settled in, but soon realized that wealth and comfort, in themselves, brought no peace. Pleasure and pain, joy and suffering still remained. Moreover, it was a lot of work to manage the servants, the budget, the cleaning and the cooking, and to take care of all the guests that suddenly started arriving to enjoy their newfound wealth.

After a year, she was ready to accompany her husband to the hermit's abandoned cottage, bringing just two changes of clothing and a pouch of herbs and spices. She, too, was ready to open her heart to the Bestower of All Gifts, and to swell, with the tiny tributary of her song, the ocean of Krishna's harmonies.

The Snake Who Lost His Hiss

*t*he elders of a village visited a much-venerated saint where he
was meditating in a cave in the mountains and complained about
Nagarajah, an evil snake who was terrorizing the village. "His hiss
can be heard for miles around," they said. "He bites and swallows our
cattle, our dogs, our children, our men, our women. Even the bravest
among us have become afraid to venture out into the fields, which are
parched, and uncultivated. Our granaries are depleted and empty. Our
numbers are dwindling from death by the snake and by starvation. Help
us, Guru. You alone can subdue and vanquish Nagarajah."

The saint, realizing the gravity of the situation, descended to the
village and went straight to a large, spreading bodhi tree. Under its
leafy canopy children had always played, yogis had meditated, and lovers had lain in each other's arms under the moonlight. But no more.
Now at its coiling, twisted roots lived Nagarajah in his burrow, like a
terrifying, tyrannical beast.

"Come forth, O Ancient One," the saint called, and the snake crept
out of his hole, slithering and undulating, his dark scales shimmering in
the sunlight. He was awesome in his length, strength, and beauty. He
glided to the Guru, coiling meekly at his feet.

"What is this I hear about you being the scourge of the village? Leave
your destructive ways. Behave yourself. Don't kill needlessly. Stop bit-

ing your neighbors and leave them alone," the saint said.

And miraculously, because Nagarajah could be made conscious of the consequences of his acts, and because he had the sense and the power to obey the saint, he returned to his burrow, resolving henceforth to leave his evil ways, and be good.

Thereafter, the fields again yielded grain, the children came out to play, the lovers loved, the brave hunters came out with their bows and their arrows, and the villagers again found themselves living in peace.

One day, several months later, the saint passed by the tree in the village, and found Nagarajah coiled near the root of the tree. The creature was utterly transformed: his scales had fallen off; he looked mangy, emaciated, innocuous, and limp; sores covered the snake's body, and he appeared on the verge of death.

"Oi, what happened to you?" the saint asked.

"This, O Guru, is the fruit of obedience, of being good. I obeyed you, I gave up my evil ways, I let the villagers alone, I stopped biting them, I stopped eating their livestock, and what happened? Look what they did to me. The children come and throw stones at me. Even the rats dance on my head. I haven't eaten for months. I am simply waiting to be eaten when I die."

The saint looked at Nagarajah without pity, and said, "This is your own fault. I told you not to bite them, but I didn't tell you not to hiss."

HERMITS

*Y*ears ago, three middle-aged relatives, two men and a woman, became fed up with their lives in a sprawling metropolis. They had had enough of the usual ways: family, children, relatives, guests, food, and money—earning, spending, bargaining, haggling, and hoarding—and above all, the inevitable and constant bantering and chattering involved in the business of living. Stifled and ill from the unremitting stress, longing for solitude and stillness, the three decided to retreat into the mountains and observe total silence. For the sake of safety, they left together in search of the place where they could begin to lead their hermetic and isolated lives.

After wandering together for over a year, they found an ideal spot in a remote region of the Himalayas, where a flowing stream, caves, fruiting trees, and edible tubers, roots, and bark gave them everything three ascetics would ever need. Here they settled down to live out the rest of their lives with the equanimity that only a life sheltered from the norm can bestow.

Soon all three of them regained their health, and with it, a sense of peace, happiness, and harmony. Living with the seasons and the forest animals and birds, listening to their sounds and songs along with the whispers of the breeze and roar of wind and waters, they practiced prayer, yoga, meditation, and contemplated the universe within and without. The three savored their solitude, which unfurled boundless spaces within them, and adored their silence, which tasted like the sweetest honey.

One day a sleek, wild stallion came into their territory, grazed a bit, and galloped off into the forest again.

"What a beautiful black stallion!" said one of the men, three months later.

"No—it was brown, not black," corrected the second hermit, after another six months had passed.

Another year elapsed, and this time it was the woman who spoke up. "If you two don't stop this endless bickering," she said angrily, "I'm going to leave!"

From the Eyes of Stars

*t*here was once a king who was very attached to his palace, from
the sprawling gardens which separated the surrounding wilderness by an intricate bronze fence, to every room in its lavish interior.

The grounds, exquisitely designed by the best landscape architects in the kingdom, boasted every class of rare plant. The king personally supervised the maintenance of the royal gardens, spending hours scolding and berating the gardeners when they neglected to pull even a single weed or forgot to trim a dead or dying flower. And indeed, set like a jewel in the loveliest of valleys, it was an exquisite garden, with hanging vines flowering one by one through all the seasons, festooning the deodars, and the leaves of horse chestnut trees luminescent like amber beads in the spring, aflame as if with candles in summer.

Inside, winding stairways and floors of precious marble imported from the best quarries in the world connected the palace's many levels. Its walls were inlaid with lovely designs in lapis lazuli and carnelian, jasper and jade. The king spent hours insuring that all was immaculate, that every crystal vase and lamp, statue and sofa was dusted and polished daily.

One late evening while the king was standing near the fence and raging against the gardeners for not pruning the rose bushes, a dirty and ragged fakir walked up to the king, and said,

"May I spend a night at this guest house?"

"Guest house!" The king roared, looking out of the barred fence, as if out of a prison cell. "Does this look like a guest house to you?"

"Yes, it does."

"Open your eyes, mendicant! This is a palace, not a guest house," the king said, turning away, half angry at himself for condescending to have this dialogue with a beggar.

"Are you sure this isn't?" The fakir persisted. "Who lived here before you did?"

"My father, Sardar Ram Singh," the king scoffed.

"And who before him?"

"My grandfather, Sardar Narayan Singh."

"And before him?"

"My great-grandfather, Buta Singh."

And the fakir did not stop questioning the king till the king had recited the names of at least twenty of his ancestors.

"Open your eyes, Majesty. If this is not a guest house, then what is it? One ruler comes here, stays for some years and passes away, and then another one comes, and so it goes. No one lives here permanently."

The king looked into the fakir's eyes, and saw stars, wheeling slowly. One of the stars became an eye, and the king found himself transposed behind it. The scroll of time unrolled rapidly, backwards through the generations, and he saw his father, and his father, and his father, and so on, back into personal prehistory. And then it extended forward in time, to the king's own body burning on the funeral pyre, his son living in the palace, and his son after him, till the end of their line. He saw the outlines of his beloved garden change, dust settle on his favorite objects of art, the walls and roof of his palace crumble into sand.

"Who are you?" the king asked the beggar, shaken by the vision.

"I am wealthy beyond measure," the fakir said. "If all my treasure were to burn to ashes, nothing of mine will be lost."

"Come," said the king, unlocking his gate. "Please come in."

But the fakir had vanished.

Leaving his gate unlocked, the king walked back to his palace, a changed man, incapable now of looking at his life and all his possessions through anything other than the eyes of stars.

STORIES FROM THE

Ramayana

Introduction to the Stories from the Ramayana

The *Ramayana*, or "Travels of Rama," is the oldest Indian epic, written by the sage Valmiki around the fifth century B.C.

Rama, the epic's hero, is another manifestation of Vishnu, who abandoned his blissful sleep on the eternal ocean of consciousness, and incarnated in order to destroy the demon king, Ravana. Rama, eldest son of Dasratha, king of Ayodhya, had three half-brothers. On the eve of Rama's succession to the throne, amidst great festivity and rejoicing, Manthara, the hunchbacked maidservant of Rama's stepmother, Kaikeyi, poisoned her mistress's heart and convinced her that the throne should go to Kaikeyi's own son, Bharata. Because Dasratha adored her and was indebted to Kaikeyi for saving his life once, he acceded to her demand, which included sending Rama into exile in the forest for fourteen years. Dasratha, devastated by his own actions, died shortly thereafter.

Rama, however, took this turn of events in his stride. Calm in adversity, knowing that what we term "misfortune" is destiny's way of fulfilling the universe's harmonious design, Rama departed Ayodhya in the company of Sita, his wife, and Lakshmana, his half-brother.

Though peace-loving and wise, Rama was profoundly disturbed when Ravana abducted Sita. He took up arms against the demon king to retrieve his beloved, aided by all the forces of the universe, including various animals.

Sita is another personification of Lakshmi, Vishnu's consort. She is an example of true, pure, and unfaltering love. Following her husband into exile, she remains fiercely faithful to Rama despite Ravana's many seductions.

Lakshmana embodies utter and unquestioning devotion to Rama and Sita, and protects the couple in their exile.

Guha is an eccentric forest king who sheltered Rama and Sita in their exile.

Ahalya, fashioned by Brahma himself in one of his erotic moments, is a beautiful woman. She is married to the sage, Gautama.

Hanuman, a monkey man, son of Vayu, Lord of the Wind, was indispensable to Rama in winning his battle with Ravana. A symbol of utter, one-pointed devotion to Rama, Hanuman is worshipped in India and many temples are devoted to him.

THE SINEWS OF HIS SPIRIT

*g*uha, the tattooed, almost naked, short, dark hunter king, didn't live by the usual laws and rules of humankind. He trusted and obeyed his own heart, did whatever he liked, whenever he liked, and moved through his days freely and spontaneously. Instead of the God or gods of the Brahmans, he worshiped trees. He never went into Ayodhya, the city where there were more people than trees, more houses and shops than boulders and animals.

The Brahmans, the priests of Ayodhya, thought Guha was a very bad example for the youth and citizens. He didn't respect or obey them or their gods. They set out to reform Guha by setting themselves up as models of behavior. They pitched fancy tents on the edge of Guha's forest, and installed a statue of Shiva under a walnut tree. Everyday they came and bathed it with coconut milk, smothered and smudged it with vermilion and sandalwood paste, offered flowers and nuts and sweets, and chanted their mantras loudly, so Guha could hear them.

"What are you doing, smearing all that stuff on a stone, and making that terrible noise?" Guha asked, returning from the hunt one day, with a dead deer slung over his shoulder.

"Worshiping, Guha, worshiping. Learn from us how to worship, for we have been ordained by Shiva himself to teach sinful mankind the proper path to salvation. You are a cruel, sinful man, a hunter, a killer, an eater of innocent animals. You can only redeem yourself by following in our footprints. Worship this Shiva, and you will be saved."

Guha said to them, "I am saved already. Don't tell me how to or what to worship. You can worship as you please, but I only worship God, and God is a tree."

The Brahmans laughed at him. "God is a tree! Pagan! Heathen! Can a tree teach you anything? Can you become wise by loving a tree? God is a tree! Guha, Guha, you are going straight to hell unless you change your ways."

"A tree is more alive than this . . . this," said Guha, instinctively giving the garlanded statue a kick. The Brahmins gasped in shock while Guha discovered to his delight that the kick felt very good. So he gave the statue another good kick. "I would rather worship dung," he said, turning away and running.

The Brahmans chased him, but he climbed a tall tree and sat safely in its branches, laughing down at them. The Brahmans waved their fists at him, swearing and cursing. But Guha only laughed the more.

"When I hug you," Guha said to the tree as he lay on one of its limbs, "I can feel your sap with the skin of my heart. You give me peace and energize me. No matter how sick I am, you heal me. You feed me and feed these wonderful animals that delight and nourish me. You give me shelter and shade, fresh air, wood for my home and my fire, and mulch for my grain. You catch the energy of the sun and send it down to the earth so it can become green and feed us with its many-colored fruits. I adore you and the forest in which you have your being, this jungle that is not a pretty little garden shaped by human will and labor, but the thing itself, God in all his terror and beauty."

The priests went away for the moment and had a conference. "Poor deluded Guha! We have to save his soul. So let's continue to worship our statue and he may learn from us by precept how to worship. He nullifies everything we stand for, so he must be reformed."

But nothing the Brahmans did changed Guha's heartfelt view. Because the kick he had given Shiva's statue felt so very good and satisfying, he resolved to kick it everyday without fail on his way back from hunting, before he went off to cook his kill and enjoy his wine. And every kick was accompanied by conversation.

"You dead and deaf old lump of rock!" he would say one day. "How can you be my God? My God is lord of the green things and the galaxies, of flowing water, hearts, and the great formless energy of the universe pulsing in everything, especially trees, which these ignorant people are cutting down to build cities in which they huddle together in their airless temples with their stone gods. This forest is the real temple. These idiots can't see that the pictures they make of their gods are only masks, reminders of god, not god. You are just a stupid stone!"

"I would rather worship myself—I see, feel, hear, and curse, unlike you, you clod!" he would say another day before greeting the statue in his usual way.

And his kicks got harder, and began to hurt his foot, but he didn't mind. He felt good as he massaged it, the pain reminding him that he hadn't succumbed to small man's small version of God's boundless, unfathomable being.

Then the monsoons came and flooded the forest. The Brahmans returned to the city, and left the statue of Shiva immersed in the muddy waters. But no matter how tired he was, and how much he had to go out of his way, on his way back from his daily hunt, Guha passed the statue of Shiva and gave it a walloping blow with his foot.

One evening when Guha approached the statue, hungry wolves encircled him before he had the chance to give it his ritual kick. His arrows were all gone, so he hurriedly climbed the walnut tree above the drowned statue. He resolved to kick the stone before the night was over, but the wolves had not yet left, so he had to continue his perch upon the tree. He had not eaten all day and was hungry. He tried to eat the nuts but they were too hard, so he began to hit the statue with them in lieu of his usual blow. He shivered, and nestled closer to the bark of the tree. At dawn the wolves left, and Guha climbed down. He was very angry with himself for having missed a day in which he did not kick Shiva.

But he did not have time to stay angry for too long. He caught a chill that night, and after a short attack of fever, died.

Yama, Lord of Death, sent his demonic messengers to bring Guha before him for judgment. One of them carried a tiny noose in his hand. He tore out Guha's soul, which was no bigger than a thumb, and tied the noose around it. Guha kicked and screamed, but it was no use. Besides, Yama's messengers respected Brahmans and hated Guha for kicking Shiva's statue. They taunted him all the way to Yama's country.

"You kicker of God! It is time for you to burn in the fires of hell. Demons are waiting to roast your soul alive and eat you. Repent, even now, and your sentence may be commuted a little. Admit you were all wrong about everything all along."

"I'll gladly suffer the fires of hell but I won't worship a God who won't accept me as he has made me, in my entirety. I have only kicked your stone statue so far, but when I meet him I will spit on his face if he is that petty," Guha replied, the sinews of his spirit surging strong within him.

At Yama's gate, guarded by fearsome dwarfs, the messengers tightened Guha's noose and began to whip him with barbed hooks to punish his insolence. One of the fearsome dwarves jumped into the fray and for once in his life Guha was truly afraid. But to his surprise, the dwarf shielded Guha from the others, and said,

"It is not his turn to die yet. Release him!"

"A traitor amongst us!" the messengers shouted, and redoubled their ferocity. It was a bloody battle in which everyone got hurt, for the messengers of death are not easily cheated of their prize. But the dwarf succeeded in snatching Guha's soul away from their fury.

Before their eyes the dwarf transformed into a white bull, with large muscular humps, dark eyes, and horns that curled up like the branches of trees. It was Nandin, shape-shifter, guardian of animals, Shiva's mount.

"He is not to go into the Land of the Dead. He will be judged by Lord Shiva himself," Nandin said, picking up Guha gently in his jaws, sheltering him in his warm, wet mouth, and bounding away.

Death's messengers laughed and rejoiced at this. "Shiva himself will roast him alive! Shiva wants this prize!"

Lord Yama, God of Death, also partial to Brahmans, couldn't wait to see and hear how Shiva would punish Guha. He hurried away to Mount Kailash, where Shiva lived. He arrived at the same time as Nandin, who tenderly dropped Guha from his mouth before Lord Shiva.

"Good," said Lord Yama. "Now we can both punish him to our heart's content."

"Punish him?" Lord Shiva asked, surprised. "What for?"

"What for? Why, don't you remember what this wild and dangerous man did to you on the edge of the forest? He is a sinner, an offender of Gods. He didn't worship you, and not only that, he insulted you. To be more specific, he kicked you many times with his foot!"

"Kicked? No, no, Yama, you have it all wrong. He came daily, without fail, to do his obeisance to me."

Yama began to say something angrily when Shiva interrupted him.

"Don't presume to know the only way to worship, Lord Yama. Guha has been a very regular and disciplined devotee of mine. He greeted me faithfully and passionately every day without fail when I came to his forest. One rainy, cold, windy night when I was drowning, he even kept a sleepless vigil to watch over me. He fasted for my sake one whole night, and even made offerings of walnuts to me when he himself didn't have anything to eat. He showered me with water, and gave me ornaments of leaves, and did not succumb to the tactics of men pretending to love me. That is why, O Yama, he is mine."

"But he thinks you are a . . . tree!" spat Lord Yama.

"Don't presume to know who or what or where I am, Lord of Death," Shiva said, reaching out and untying the noose around Guha's soul. Guha ran up to Shiva and hugged him, like he hugged his trees, his breast next to the bark, feeling its sap against the skin of his heart. He looked up, and found himself perched upon Vishala, Narayana's World Tree. Its roots were Brahma, its trunk Shiva, its branches Vishnu. In its branches, spread into infinity, nested galaxies. Its fruit were whirling worlds, and its leaves were songs.

The Lord of Death was extremely angry. He felt cheated of his soul. He reached out to pluck Guha from Shiva's embrace, but Shiva sheltered him in his massive arms. "It is not time for him to die just yet, but to return to life. It is his destiny to save the earth and its trees, and protect the heroes that will have to take shelter in the forest, like endangered seeds, from the stupidity of man." Shiva's eye scanned forward in time, and saw Rama, Lakshmana and Sita taking refuge with Guha in their exile.

Guha found himself back in his body, back on the earth, back in his forest.

"But what . . . what," Lord Yama was trying to say through his uncontrollable rage, "what about all those people whose only God is a stone statue? Are they all wrong? Misled? Deluded?"

"I am in all things, Yama, including stone. It is not what they worship, but how sincerely and passionately they worship, that brings them to me."

Back on earth, Guha returned to his favorite temple beneath the walnut tree. Shiva's statue was almost drowned by now. Guha felt for it with his hands, hauled it up from the mud, put it on his shoulders, and took it home: there to worship, and every now and then, kick it.

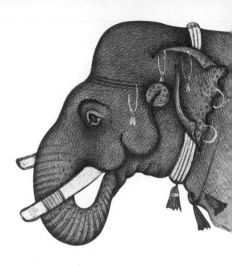

ASHES AND DUST

halya and Gautama were childhood friends who loved each other dearly. They played together every day of the year. And because young Gautama was devoted to Vishnu and Lakshmi from an early age, the children would fashion small, shapeless clay statues of the god and goddess, place them in temples of brick and stone, and worship them together. When they grew up, Ahalya and Gautama married, and after a few years moved into the forest outside the city of Mithila to live as rishis, sages, in the lap of nature, which they believed would be more conducive to a spiritual life.

Together the couple built a small hut of mud and thatch by a stream of crystal clear turquoise waters that coursed through white marble boulders upon jewel-like cobblestones. A meadow matted with delicate alpine flowers rolled down to the edge of thick forests of tall oak trees. Rabbits, gazelles, and colorful birds, pheasants, magpies, and sweet-tongued thrushes all came to eat from Ahalya and Gautama's hands. Not far away, a serene lake, like a clear eye, reflected everything that came within its ambit. Their life was harmonious, peaceful and idyllic for many years, and would have continued this way had Ahalya's beauty not complicated and destroyed it.

Over the years Gautama, because of his one-pointed devotion to Vishnu and Lakshmi, became a powerful sage who gained control over his passions. He kept Vishnu and Lakshmi in his heart like a sacred seed of fire, and lived a life of yoga and prayer. Daily he implored, "Vishnu, Lord of the World, Lakshmi, Mother, Energy of the World, come,

come into our home and our hearts!" And though Ahalya joined him in the prayer, offering flowers, lighting the incense, and ringing the bell, many times her attention lay somewhere else. A dark desire stirred in her depths and in her dreams like behemoths beneath the sea.

Every morning Ahalya would set out to bathe in the still lake behind their cottage. There she would be reminded as she sat on the banks and gazed at her own reflection, of how lovely she was. Brahma himself had created her in a moment of erotic passion. Her long, dark hair fell in waves about her face, framing exquisitely chiseled features: liquid, languid eyes, a mouth full and sensuous beneath a perfectly proportioned nose. Her body, too, in her deerskin and tree bark, was beautifully proportioned, from the tips of her hair to the ends of her toes.

During these moments Ahalya would reflect, "I am fit for the gods. I am wasting away in the forest. Even Gautama, whom I love dearly, is as a brother to me now, and has eyes only for nature's beauty, which reminds him of the beauty of his gods. His blood has turned to sap. I wish for someone more passionate than he, someone with more heat in his veins than my husband has."

After having fulfilled his household duties, Gautama wished only to retreat within himself and explore the universe there. While Ahalya, too, had a strong spiritual side, she possessed equally intense carnal longing and ambitions. At times she was full of a deep content, but at times she grew weary of wisdom, and the clarity of her vision was clouded by the sediment of her ego, especially on those days when Gautama preoccupied himself with other holy matters and could not give her the attention she craved. In these moments, Ahalya would sit at the lake's edge and visualize the kind of man who would come to make love to her: how he would look, and look at her; the way he would approach, and touch her.

The formless plasma of the universe began to take shape into a body that would fulfill her desires. And he in whose loins the desire found its echo was none other than the god, Indra. Someone on earth was calling to him, and he had to go. He looked down from his clouds, saw Ahalya, and was immediately inflamed by passion.

Late one afternoon while Gautama was out collecting roots and tubers for their dinner, chopping wood, bathing, and supplicating Vishnu and Lakshmi with the offerings of freshly plucked flowers to visit their home and hearts, Indra took a sip of soma, assumed the form of Gautama, and swaggered his way to the couple's cottage.

Ahalya's body quickened at the sight of his approaching form. In his clean, crisp dhoti, his moustache and beard trimmed and recently washed, he looked effulgent in the last rays of the setting sun. Her insight revealed to her at once that this was not Gautama, but Indra in disguise.

As Indra came to the door, an image formed from her dreams, any qualms she may have had melted away in her knowledge of who this was. What a lineage! What beauty! What power! What fame! This was no ordinary mortal, but a god!

Her emotions blazed as Ahalya looked into her lover's eyes. Because he came in a familiar form, because Ahalya had been made ready by her longing for just this moment, because the desire was longstanding, and now mutual, there was no hiatus between their seeing each other and their meeting. In a conflagration of arousal, they explored and touched and consummated their passion, again and again. The clandestine and illicit circumstance of their sexuality added to their ardor.

"Go," Ahalya would whisper in Indra's ear. "Go now, hurry!" But no sooner would he move away than their inflamed fervor drew them together again and they lost themselves in their ecstasy.

By and by, as the sun began to set, Gautama returned from his evening prayers with flowers in his hands. He opened the cottage door and stood in shock at the sight of his half-naked wife in the embrace of another, who looked just like him. It didn't take him long to know who this was, and what had happened.

In a fit of rage, with all the power of his austerities behind him, he cursed Indra.

"You, who call yourself a god, but have no control over your impulses, may you grow a thousand phalluses all over your body so everyone may see the true face of your concupiscence!"

Right there and then a thousand penises thrust out of Indra's pores. Everywhere, upon his face and ears and head, neck and chest and arms, hands and legs and feet dangled pudenda that left him a hideous sexual monster. Indra scurried away in shame, to hide his gross and comical body.

God or no, Indra's indiscretions would not be easily dismissed. Brahma saw to that. For a thousand years Indra would be forced to do penance and reflect upon his uncontrollable and immoral appetites. Over those centuries, Indra resolved to control himself in the future, so Brahma took pity on him, transforming his many penises into eyes. Instead of indulging in pleasures, for the next thousand years he watched the drama of life. But because he was immortal and ever youthful, his passions returned, and he began his pendulum swing between abstinence and indulgence all over again.

In the meantime, on earth, Gautama turned to Ahalya, his heart burning in agony, and said, "And you, wife—and yet no wife, for you have betrayed the basic trust of our marriage— may your burning in unholy desire for another incinerate you to ash!"

Ahalya had no time even to plead with her husband. Flames rose around her, licking her beautiful body with tongues of fire, her tender toes and tight thighs, flat belly and firm breasts, long neck, luscious lips, pert nose, long eyelashes, and lustrous hair—all afire, and soon charred and consumed to ash.

As Gautama stood, watching his wife's transformation, he felt his own heart turn to cinders at the sight before him. For in loving someone, one becomes the other, and whatever one does to the other, one does to oneself.

In a fit of compassion for himself and Ahalya, he amended his curse: "Thousands of years from now, Vishnu and Lakshmi shall come in their incarnation of Rama and Sita, and when their holy feet touch your remains, Ahalya, you will be forgiven and become whole again."

Turning his back on the pile that had been his wife, Gautama shut the cottage door, and wandered out into the world. The wild flowers and grasses in the surrounding meadows wilted, the leaves on the trees and the bushes turned yellow and fell, the stream's waters dwindled and stopped flowing, the birds with their varied colored plumage flew off into the silent forest.

Inside their hut for the next thousand years, Ahalya lay in darkness. Though her body was a pile of ashes, consciousness remained in it, like a spark. She remained excruciatingly aware of her condition, with every memory intact. For a millennium she lived without her senses and her appetites. There was time enough now for regret, shame, guilt, remorse, and fury. Ahalya cursed her fate, her desire, Indra, and Gautama. She blamed Brahma for giving her beauty and desires and then punishing her for fulfilling them. She hoped for the arrival of her saviors, Rama and Sita, but doubted they existed—or if they did, that they would rescue a transgressor such as she. Ahalya also longed deeply for her companion and friend, Gautama, who never came.

After her rage spent itself, Ahalya took stock of her life. She was a pile of pulverized particulate matter on the floor of a dilapidated hut. She asked herself, "how did I get here?" The answer made her aware of her own responsibility for her present situation. She had caused her own tragedy. This admission was the beginning of her transformation back to humanness. It did, however, take another thousand years, a concatenation of other insights, and help from the deities of the universe to re-achieve it.

Ahalya determined, instead of suffering unconsciously as she had been doing, to accept her ordeal willingly, and embrace the sorrows that she had brought upon herself. So for another thousand years she burnt in the purgatorial fires that cleanse and heal.

And when she was ready, her ashes received another blessed thought: if the seeds of her carnal desires had germinated when she watered them with her attention, her spiritual desires too would bear fruit if she nurtured them with focus and longing. And a long forgotten prayer arose from the depths of her heart: "Vishnu and Lakshmi, come! Come! Come into my home and my heart!"

And as Ahalya's days wore on, now with hope and anticipation, chinks appeared in the windows and doors of the cottage, through which rays of light streamed onto the ground where she lay.

So it was that one day, weary from their wanderings in their exile, Rama and Sita came upon Ahalya and Gautama's cottage. "Oh, what a beautiful cottage!" Sita said, flinging open the door and entering. "Yes, we could live here for a while." And as Sita and Rama stepped into the hut, the dust from their feet mingled with Ahalya's ashes, and like a flame appearing suddenly from smoke, behold, the ashes became a woman again—new, shining, and pure!

Ahalya fell at Rama and Sita's feet, tears streaming from her eyes. She took the dust from their feet and put it in the parting of her own hair, saying, "Keep me always in touch with the dust of your feet, my Lord and Lady."

Then Rama lifted her up, and to Ahalya's amazement, both deities bent down and touched her feet in return, saying, "We bow to the suffering that brings God into our homes and hearts. May there always be shelter for us in the hearts of devotees cleansed through suffering."

Ahalya looked over Sita's shoulder, and there, framed in the doorway, stood Gautama, her companion, her mate, her soul—he who had prayed for thousands of years for Vishnu and Lakshmi to come and redeem his wife, so they might be reunited. Ahalya's heart was full to

overflowing with gratitude and hope.

In his hand Gautama held a freshly made broom. Sita took it from him, and began to sweep the dirt floor. She scooped up the ashes, the compost of Ahalya's suffering, and in her cupped hands, carried them outside and scattered them to the winds. As they fell back to the earth in a shower of white and grey flecks, meadow grasses sprang to life again, and the wilted flowers raised their tiny crowns and began to bloom. Seeds of trees deep in the ground stirred, germinated, and grew, bringing forth blossom and fruit. The rabbits, gazelles, vibrant birds, and other creatures returned, gamboling and drinking from the stream that flowed again with its exultant gurgling. And when Ahalya looked at her cottage, its rustic beauty and coziness were restored as well. The kitchen shone with clean utensils, the floors were covered with mats of reeds, the beds with soft furs.

And there they lived—all four of them—humans and their godlike hosts together, until a year later when it was time for Rama and Sita to move on. But even then the four were never more separated, for Rama and Sita dwelt forever like divine sparks in Ahalya and Gautama's hearts as they lived out the rest of their lives in contentment, worship, and praise.

THE TOAD WHO
DIDN'T CROAK

*t*ired, hungry, and dirty from their wanderings, Rama and Lakshmana searched for water to slake their thirst and refresh their bodies with a bath.

"I don't think there is any water here," Lakshmana said. "We have been wandering for days. I doubt that the lake we were told about even exists."

"Be patient. It does. And we will soon be there," Rama replied.

"How can you be so sure?"

"When adversity finds us, all our wisdom, like grain in a sieve, flies out of our souls, and we are left with the chaff of doubt. Share your thoughts with me, Little Brother."

"I have been very troubled in my mind, Rama. I can't shake the thought that when we were exiled by our stepmother, Kaikeyi, so that her son could inherit your throne, we should have fought for your rights. You are the legitimate king."

"Yes. But father had to honor his promise to Kaikeyi. I would not have wanted our father to break his word, Lakshmana."

"But what is a word? Air."

"Promises are stepping stones on the path of dharma. It is of such airy threads that honor is made. The universe would not be without laws, Lakshmana. It is laws that sustain the heavenly bodies and our earth. Humans, too, have laws, which we may not break without dire harm to ourselves and others. Without a commitment to dharma, Lakshmana, all our paths are lost, and humanity itself is sacrificed."

"Humanity! What humanity did Kaikeyi show? She allowed herself to be lured by that demonic woman, Manthara, who moves about the palace all humped over like a malformed lump, a dark shadow, working its poison even during the day."

"It is the shape and voice of the ego, Lakshmana, which, cut off from the general good, wants gain only for its small and illusory self. Manthara has never forgiven me for shooting a harmless arrow playfully into her hump once when we were both children. And her revenge is merely the trigger for the unraveling of a vast design, to which we ultimately have to surrender."

"Surrender! We were cowards to simply let her will prevail. If we hadn't allowed all that madness to happen, then we might still be in our palace in Ayodhya. You would be king and Sita would be queen, instead of Ravana's prisoner. Our entire lives would have been different. Better. Less full of hardship."

"Surrender to this adversity, brother, to what is, and you will see how sweet it is. It had to be."

"Nothing has to be, Rama!"

"Oh, my brother, that is not the way to peace."

"But I don't want peace! I want you to be king!"

"Without peace there is no truth, Lakshmana. Truth lives in stillness."

"I don't care for stillness. I want to be back in Ayodhya, rejoicing at your coronation!"

Lakshmana's belligerence was new. He had always been soft-spoken and obedient to Rama's will, knowing that his brother was an incarnation of Vishnu. Rama's name was on every lip that believed and trusted in God. Lakshmana, too, worshiped and adored his older brother. But fatigue had overwhelmed his brain, roiled and clouded his vision, and made him angry and despairing.

They walked in silence for a while, Lakshmana fuming inwardly at the sight of Rama's feet, full of dust, cracks, blisters, sores. "Did you never feel anything? Your coronation was the next day, you were happy, you had won Sita of the little feet and delicate ankles. To have the throne snatched from under you! And as if that wasn't enough, to be exiled for fourteen years!"

"Know, Lakshmana, that we have small minds that cannot see the whole picture, just individual events. Things do not "happen," they simply are, as the course of events in a book with the past, present, and future all laid out, always happening, always ending and beginning again. Our story is already over, Lakshmana; all our adversity has already passed away. Think of all your past sorrows. Where are they now? If you knew then that they would pass away into oblivion, as you know now that they did, you would have moved through that suffering with equanimity. This is our task here, Lakshmana, not to gain some spurious comfort and happiness, but to move into that Self within us, always present and deathless, that is our true home. Look, Lakshmana."

Lakshmana had been so preoccupied by the noises in his head that he didn't see they had arrived at their destination. Just as Rama finished speaking, through a clearing in the forest they came upon the lake that they sought. A chorus of frogs sang loudly. The cool and placid waters, so pellucid that they could see all the way to the pattern of the pebbles at the bottom, shimmered in the sunlight.

Rama and Lakshmana drove their bows into the earth to stand them up against a tree. Rama's bow encountered a rock in the forest floor, so he pulled it out of the ground, and then a short distance away in the mud, plunged it deep into the earth.

The two took off their quivers and then their clothes, drank their fill of the cool and sweet water, and went in for a swim. Rama dove in first, and in no time swam to the middle of the lake.

As Lakshmana stepped into the lake, he still didn't understand the convoluted logic of struggle and surrender, free will and destiny. He wished he had as much clarity as Rama did, but then Rama, being Vishnu, was in tune with the intricacies of the universe. Lakshmana said to himself: "I will ask him how one knows when to accept and when to fight."

As he walked deeper into the waters, he heard Rama's voice in his head. "When our passions become as still as this lake, when we are detached from Maya, from the illusion of our own lives, we shall hear the voice that tells us when to struggle and when to surrender."

As Lakshmana submerged his head into the waters, all the turmoil seething in him like cobras stinging his organs, all his questions and quandaries dissolved, and a quiet peace took their place. In that silence was a little kernel that stood apart from and above the joys and sorrows, hopes and travails of his life, a point of utter stillness in which his world, though apparently in shambles, was supremely all right. His being expanded to include a long forgotten joy. And from the eye of that joy, he perceived how everything that had happened was as inevitable as lines and colors in a perfect and complete design.

He looked over at Rama, now seemingly asleep upon the waters, like Vishnu, a smile upon his sacred lips, his brow high and broad above his beloved features. All his love, obscured by the clouds of misfortune, returned as a tide, reversing the ebb within Laksmana's heart. How dearly he worshiped Rama! How deeply he admired and adored him for being at once human and divine; for his ability to always transcend the fickle circumstances of his life; for the clarity of his vision and the trust he placed in the workings of the universe; for letting vicissitudes move through him, like the wind through a harp.

Lakshmana knew that this was what he himself could become: the very zenith of humanhood, the very flower of the conflicted and marvelous human animal. Rama was what Lakshmana strove to be in the best of times; even in the worst, Rama guided him like a blind man's staff.

Emerging from the waters, they dried themselves, and put on their clothes. Pulling out his bow from the marsh, Rama noticed that the tip was stained with blood. Rama said, "Look, Lakshmana, I'm afraid I have injured some creature."

Lakshmana dug into the earth with his hands, and brought out a toad covered with mud and blood, breathing rapidly, the air sac beneath his chin billowing in and out, his large, protruding eyes bulging in pain. The end of Rama's bow had pierced through his body, and he lay in Lakshmana's hand, dying.

Stricken with pain at the sight before him, Rama cried to the toad: "Why didn't you croak? You croak loudly enough when you are in the jaws of a snake."

"O Lord," the toad said, "When I am attacked by a snake, I struggle in his mouth, I croak loudly and cry to you, 'O Rama, save me! Save me, Rama!' But this time I found that it was Rama himself who was killing me, so what could I do?"

Rama extended his hands towards Lakshmana, who placed the toad gently in his cupped hands.

"There's only one thing sweeter than dying by Rama's hand," the toad said, softly. "To die in Rama's hands."

HANUMAN BARES ALL

hanuman's mother was an apsara, a heavenly being, cursed to be a monkey, and his father was Vayu, the Lord of the Winds. As an infant, this child of heaven and earth thought the sun was a big fruit in the sky, and sprang up to pluck it; Brahma promised he would be invincible in battle and declared to Indra that his bolts would never harm Hanuman.

Hanuman, the white monkey man, combined the best of animal, human being, and god. His simian body was very useful to him in traversing long distances in the service of Rama, leaping from limb to limb among the trees, and loping with long strides on the ground. Claws, paws, fur, and tail were all indispensable to him in his many adventures. At the same time he stood erect, used his hands for manipulative tasks, and taught himself grammar and the rules of language, and communicated through reading, writing, speech, arithmetic, algebra and geometry. He was equally capable of expressing himself through loud howls as through articulate poetry, song, and music.

Hanuman possessed a natural spirit of inquiry and curiosity that led him into the sciences. Through his formidable moral sense, he knew that wickedness had to be confronted, fought, and destroyed. Well versed in the scriptures, he recited them by heart, parsing and interpreting them rationally and with feeling. Hanuman's divine origins enabled him to defy gravity and fly freely through infinite spaces; his terrestrial skills allowed him to live with awareness, enjoy the fruits of the earth, and walk upon it with every inch of his soles touching the ground.

Hanuman was crucial to Rama in his battle against evil. When the ten-head Ravana, charismatic king of Lanka, abducted Sita, Hanuman's voice lent hope to both Sita and Rama. He mobilized the army of animals—monkeys, bears, and birds—that would help Rama win Sita back. When the animals despaired of ever finding Sita's whereabouts, Hanuman located her in the island of Lanka, hidden in Ravana's palace. Disguised as a cat, he gathered information, found Sita, and offering Rama's ring, convinced her he was Rama's envoy. When Ravana's spies caught him and set his tail on fire, he ingeniously used his punishment to set Lanka ablaze before quenching the flames by dipping it in the ocean. He helped build the bridge to Lanka so that the allies could cross over and rescue Sita. Bearing Rama on his shoulders, the monkey man leapt across the ocean to Lanka.

Hanuman flew all the way to the Himalayas to fetch healing herbs when Rama lay dying on the battlefield. When he couldn't identify them, he uprooted the entire mountain and carried it resting on the palm of his hand to Lanka, where a physician could choose the correct herbs and heal Rama.

It was the monkey man's devotion, service and unwavering love of Rama that distinguished Hanuman, earned him the stature of a god, and assured a place for him in the hearts and minds of men, women and children of India and South East Asia.

Our story occurs at the end of the Ramayana, after the demon Ravana had been fought and killed, Sita had been rescued, and Rama had regained his kingdom.

To celebrate the victory and the reuniting of the lovers, a huge feast was held, in which all the animals who had served Rama caroused and feasted on the tastiest of fruits, honey, meats and wine. It was time for them to return to their own habitations in caves and forests, and they were all sad to part with Rama, the incarnation of Vishnu in human form.

Rama thanked them in a brilliant speech, emphasizing the help that he received from the animal kingdom in accomplishing his phenomenal feats. He assured them he would always be there for them in times of need. The connection, he said, was eternal and unbreakable. And then he gave them all rich and beautiful gifts.

Finally he called Hanuman, and said, "Without your strength, devotion, and loyalty I would have been lost, Hanuman. I can never repay

you, or do or say anything to express my gratitude to you. But as a small token of my appreciation, please take this."

Rama removed a bracelet that he had worn through the entire course of epic events, and handed it to Hanuman. All gathered there gasped with surprise. What an honor! Rama's own bracelet! So valuable it was that Hanuman could now buy a kingdom with it and retire. The bracelet featured numerous, huge, flawless emeralds, rubies and diamonds.

The monkey man took the gift, examined it carefully, turning it round and round in his paw. He squeezed it, so that some of the precious stones popped out of their settings. He took each one of them, held them up against the light and squinted at them, eyeing each one closely as if looking for something. He even stuffed some of the gems in his cheek pouches, cracked them with his teeth, spat them out again into the palm of his hand, and looked inside. He looked disappointed, as if whatever it was he was looking for wasn't there. He then broke apart the gold band and looked inside it from every possible angle. Shaking his head, he put the pieces back in the palm of Rama's hand.

"I don't want this. It is a worthless gift," said Hanuman.

The crowd of animals gasped. Here was Hanuman, who they all respected, behaving just like a monkey. Did he have any idea of the value of the gift Rama had so generously given him? What did Hanuman want? And how dare he insult Rama this way?

"What good is it?" Hanuman said, loudly.

"What good are you?" Jambavan, the bear, cried out angrily. "You receive the best gift of all, Rama's own bracelet that has been near his skin for so many years! And you call it worthless. It is you who are worthless, you old monkey!"

"Nowhere on it or in it did I find Rama's name," Hanuman said. "What good is anything without his name?"

"You don't have his name anywhere on you. Do you have any worth?"

"Oh, yes, I do! I do!" said Hanuman.

Hanuman placed the fingers of his paws just beneath his rib cage, dug them deep inside, ripped open his skin, and parted the flaps of flesh on either side, baring the large, pulsing muscle of his heart. And there upon every fiber of that organ was written "Rama! Rama! Rama!" And his heart, too, with its every beat, diastole and systole, sang "Rama! Rama! Rama!"

"This," Hanuman said, looking into Rama's eyes, misted with tears, "is far more precious to me than any thing you might give me, Lord. As the richest gift of all, promise me that you will remain here, like this, till the last beat of my heart."

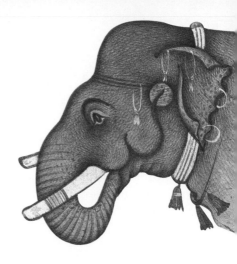

The Lowly, Holy Staff

One day while roaming in the jungles of the Himalayas with his army, Vishwamitra, warrior king of Kanya-Kubja, happened upon a quaint hermitage by a river. Looking at it, he felt transported to a different world, in which he felt completely present and alive; all weariness from his weighty responsibilities fell away. He saw many ascetics meditating in such utter stillness that they were indistinguishable from the boulders and trees against which they sat. The garden, with its exquisite arrangement of the random and the planned, seemed designed by a divine gardener in a manner beyond human capability. The plants and even the rocks were sentient, and there was no distinction between animate and inanimate, men and beasts. Men mingled with animals, sheep grazed alongside dozing tigers, trees bore fruit even in the winter. But above all, Vishwamitra was amazed by the peace of the place. It was so thick that it was almost palpable. It surrounded and entered him like a dense cloud of silence and stillness.

He knew at once that this was the ashram of the holiest of sages, Vasistha, whose attunement to the universe's creative force brought peace and well-being to his entire kingdom.

Vishwamitra got off his horse, his ivory and gold scepter studded with jewels in his hand. Leaving his army behind, he humbly approached the sage who sat under a spruce tree, deep in meditation.

Vasistha opened his eyes, and recognizing the sovereign, he arose and welcomed him warmly. The venerable sage valued his peace and silence above all, but did not complain when it was interrupted by a visitor. His insight saw the inevitability of even the most seemingly haphazard and accidental circumstance. It was Vasistha's nature to flow as water flows, seamlessly, under and over and around any obstacle it may encounter.

The two sat together, rishi and warrior king, the royal visitor asking the sage many questions, and inquiring about the well-being of all the hermits in the ashram. Vasistha offered the king divine peaches, bananas, mangoes, almonds, and cashew nuts from his orchard. The king enjoyed them all, delighted and amazed that such a haven could exist on earth, and in his very own kingdom. But the hermits' huts were humble, made of mud and wattles, and Vishwamitra silently resolved to send Vasistha a caravan of amenities: carpets for the floor; oil lamps; perhaps some horses; and servants to fell timber, fetch firewood and water, and cook for the sage.

And all too soon, it was time for Vishwamitra to leave. The king didn't want to, for the bliss he felt in the hermitage was like salve to his overworked spirit, much mauled by the many obligations of a responsible and diligent head of state. But his many duties were pressing upon him. Reluctantly he rose, bowing deeply to Vasistha.

"Wait, King," the sage said. "Bring your army inside. They look hungry and tired, and I would like to feed them."

"Oh no," said the king. "It's a huge and hungry army! It will cost you too much work. Some other time, kind sage."

"No, no, now. It will be no trouble at all," Vasistha said, bidding the generals and their men to enter. They trooped in to the clanking of armor and rustling of uniforms.

"Surabhi!" Vasistha called. By and by, the particles of air around Vasistha became visible, a swirling cloud-shape of light, which in no time coalesced into the form of a shimmering cow.

Vishwamitra's eyes grew wide and incredulous at the magic before his eyes and the miracle of the cow's phenomenal beauty. Her large and liquid eyes glowed like dark globes in her white face which shone like the full moon beneath her ebony horns. Her body and shanks glinted with velvet light. Her udders were abundant and full, as if Earth with all her bounty had materialized before his very eyes.

"Surabhi, child, we have a famished army here. Feed them."

Right then and there a feast, a gastronomical marvel, appeared before them, and the entire army fell to it and ate the various delights ravenously. Vishwamitra, too, indulged with pleasure, reeling from the deliciousness of the food and the wine, the likes of which he had never tasted. He watched his soldiers satisfy themselves, nourished to the marrow in their bones. Vasistha, too, watched them eating, like a mother hen her brood, and took joy and happiness in the sight.

"Who . . . what is she?" the king asked, when he had retrieved his tongue from speechless amazement.

"Kamadhenu, the cow of plenty," Vasistha explained, looking at her with great affection. "When the gods churned the primeval ocean to separate the poison from the nectar, she emerged from the depths of the waters. The gods gave her to us as a gift, and she has been here ever since. Oh, she is our Mother from whom all bounty flows! She is our heart, our spirit, our soul, without which we would be as children lost in the forest. And, dear King, she is as a daughter to me, feeding and sustaining us all."

Vishwamitra, who till this moment had felt nothing lacking in his life, was now suddenly filled with overwhelming desire for the magical animal. He could not live without the cow, he resolved, and nothing was going to keep him from having her.

"Great sage," he began, "you are an enlightened being, and have no desires. I am a king and a warrior, and therefore have many needs for my subjects and myself. This magical cow of yours, Holy One, truly belongs with the king. Ask what you want in return for her."

"Nothing at all, sire. She is not for sale."

"Everything has its price," the king continued, not at all discouraged. "A thousand cows and a trunk full of gold?"

"No, sire. Try to understand. You cannot have her. She belongs with us and cannot be parted from us. This can never happen. So please desist from asking for the impossible."

"You are my subject!" The king grasped his scepter. "And it is your duty . . ."

Vasistha said, calmly, "King, not all your treasury can pay for her. You cannot part her from me. She is as much mine as my skin, my heart, my stomach. You cannot take anything from me, for everything I have and own is inseparable from who I am."

"If you don't give her to me," the king said, putting his hand on his sword, "I shall take her by force."

"If you were to take her by force, she would cease to be Kamadhenu, the cow of plenty. She is the manifestation of the purity of the yogi's soul, King, and not to be bartered like common goods. Please try to understand what I am saying: she belongs to all the pure souls collectively. Become a pure soul, and she shall belong to you as she belongs to all of us here."

But his lust for the cow of plenty made the king deaf to the sense of Vasistha's words. He turned to his army, and said, "Capture her!"

Vasistha stood aside calmly in his trust that nothing was going to happen that was not meant to.

The king's men grabbed Surabhi, but in their hands she reverted back to the nebula of which she was made. The soldiers were left with shimmering particles in their hands.

"Order her to come to me!" Vishwamitra shouted at Vasistha, and when the sage said he was powerless to do so, he ordered his army to attack the rishi. Just as the horde approached Vasistha, he opened his mouth and exhaled. And the flames from his mouth turned them all to ashes.

Livid, helpless, and blind with greed, the king returned to his palace in the city, vowing to have his way. As the days went by, he lost all desire to rule. He roamed aimlessly in his well-arranged gardens

and the luxurious halls of his palace, disenchanted with all his wealth and his many possessions. None of it gave him any joy or solace. A pall descended upon him that turned all his power to dust.

His defeat at Vasistha's hands kept raging in his breast, and he wanted his revenge. So Vishwamitra relinquished his kingdom to his son, and went into the forest to perform austerities. His aim was to gain the boon of powerful weapons from Shiva with which to outdo his enemy, the great Vasistha.

For a thousand years he stood on one leg without food and water, and when Shiva appeared before him with the offer of a boon, Vishwamitra, without hesitation, said: "Grant me the finest instruments of war, the most effective weapons created by the gods, Shiva."

With his stockpile of state-of- the- art weapons, Vishwamitra wasted no time in returning to the hermitage. Without any warning, he launched a mortar on Vasistha's hut. Sizzling fire and exploding, it charred the hut to cinders.

When the smoke cleared, however, Vishwamitra saw that wild birds and other animals nearby paid little attention to him, his weapons, or the explosion. Hermits in other parts of the complex sat in the same postures as they had, as still as ever, either as composed as ever or dead in their lotus positions. Vishwamitra hoped for the latter.

From the shambles of the hut something stirred: Vishwamitra made out a burnt figure coming forth. With loincloth charred, singed hair standing on end, and a face blackened with the blast, Vasistha came towards him, armed with a wooden staff in his hand. Vishwamitra laughed at the sight of the battered sage in a seared loincloth with a puny staff in his hand.

But Vasistha was not intimidated. Planting his staff firmly and steadily before him, straight and tall like the world axis, he faced the erstwhile king and prepared to speak. Vishwamitra, furious to see the sage still alive, pulled out from his quiver a poisoned arrow made of flint from Mars, which Shiva had assured the king never missed its mark.

Hissing and spluttering the arrow went straight for Vasistha's heart. But the wooden staff in his hand, now incandescent with a quiet energy, became a wide shield off which the arrow bounced before falling limply to the ground.

Enraged, Vishwamitra resorted to his deadliest weapons, detonating them with a powerful blast. No one and nothing could survive this. When the air cleared, however, he saw Vasistha remained standing, fragments of the weapons swirling in pieces around the stately staff.

In a final effort, Vishwamitra ignited all his projectiles at once, aiming them this time at Vasistha's staff. But as they flew at it, the staff gaped open, revealing a vast, elemental space, the Milky Way undulating through it, and all the king's explosives turned into stars in the darkness.

"And now," said Vasistha, as Vishwamitra stood there, all his weapons spent, "Since you have destroyed my peace, I am going to kill you!" He lifted his staff into the air, and was about to bring it down on Vishwamitra's head when all the sages in the hermitage who had been quietly meditating through it all, cried out in unison: "Vasistha! Stop! Remember who you are. Remember why we have Kamadhenu! Don't respond to force with force! Let him go! Return to your Self, great sage. Return to your bliss!"

Vasistha lowered his staff, centered its axis along the midline of his body, aligned himself, standing erect and motionless behind it as a pillar, and instantly calmed down. Regaining his former bearing of tranquility and warmth, the sage turned to Vishwamitra, and said, "May your journey to yourself be successful, King. May your great rage become the motivation of your enlightenment." The venerable rishi then quietly returned to his place beneath the tree, sat in the lotus position, and resumed his meditation.

Humiliated beyond words, disenchanted with his weapons, his failure knocking violently against the shores of his ambitious, vengeful heart, Vishwamitra cried out: "A staff! A mere wooden staff has defeated me! What good are all the weapons of the gods against his little piece of wood!"

And a longing arose in his heart to get Vasistha's staff for himself; but, before it could take a hold in his heart, the sense of Vasistha's earlier words drifted into his consciousness: "Nothing I have is separate from who I am."

In a flash Vishwamitra understood how hopeless it was to attempt to wrest anything from the sage. He knew he must now turn and find the true source of the sage's powers, and that his own journey to himself had just begun.

STORIES FROM THE
MAHABHARATA

Introduction to the Stories from the Mahabharata

*t*he *Mahabharata*, from which the following five stories have been adapted, is one of the two great epics of the Hindus, the other being the *Ramayana*. Its date is uncertain, but one estimate puts it as far back as the fifth century B.C. 'Mahabharata' means 'The Great War of the (race of) Bharatas,' or 'The Great War.' In 220,000 lines – which make it the longest poem of the world—it depicts the bitter feud between two brothers' families: the Kauravas and the Pandavas.

Dhritrashtra, the Kauravas' patriarch, was the elder of the two brothers, but because he was born blind, his younger brother, Pandu, head of the Pandavas, succeeded him as king. Though the two brothers loved each other dearly, their sons go to battle for the throne.

Among Dhritrashtra's hundred sons, the eldest, Duryodhana, intent on securing the throne for himself alone, refuses to share the empire with the Pandavas. To this end he schemes to kill Pandu's five sons: Yudhishtra, Arjuna, Bheem, Sahdeva and Nakula. Though he fails at his, Duryodhana manages to oust his cousins from the kingdom through trickery – a game of loaded dice – banishing them to a life in the forest for thirteen years.

The Pandavas at first comply, but after their repeated efforts at family reconciliation fail, they wage war upon their cousins, the Kauravas. With Krishna's guidance, the Pandavas claim victory, and go on to rule successfully for thirty-six years.

In an intriguing aside within the *Mahabharata*, all five Pandava brothers are married to and live together with the same woman, Draupadi. This unusual arrangement comes about after Arjuna, a master archer, returns home after having won Draupadi in a contest. He calls out, "Mother, come see what I have won!" His mother, who hasn't noticed the maiden, replies, "Whatever it is, Arjuna, share it equally with your brothers!" Honoring their mother's wish, all five marry Draupadi.

Krishna, the Blue God, an incarnation of Vishnu, is cousin to the Pandavas from their mother's side. Transcending the imperatives of a warrior, Krishna serves as Arjuna's charioteer in the war, speaking to him as his Higher Self, and instructing him in the portion of the *Mahabharata* known as the *Bhagawad Gita*.

THE DEER PEOPLE

Unlike his brother Yudhishtra, who was introspective and gentle, Bheem, the second of the Pandava brothers, was a passionate man. He was physically strong, loving, and loyal to his family. Believing revenge to be a sacred duty, he broke the backs of demons and his enemies against his knees.

And Bheem loved to eat. Of whatever food the Pandavas hunted and gathered, half was given to Bheem, and the rest divided amongst his four brothers and wife. Though he would eat any and every thing, meat was his favorite food, for it satisfied his massive hunger. He was always hungry after eating leaves and fruit, his stomach growling, his mind discontent and searching. But a young doe grilled on the fire in its own fat and juices was delicious and tided him over well till his next meal.

One morning, as Bheem awoke from a heavy slumber after a great meal of roasted deer, he saw his brother, Yudhishtra, sitting under a tree with his hands on his forehead. Bheem slapped him on his back affectionately, and said, "What's the matter? Had another of your disturbing dreams, brother?"

"This was no dream. In the early hours of this morning, when the morning stars were still shedding their light on the forest, the deer people came to me."

"The deer people? Never met them," said Bheem, humoring his brother.

"Because you couldn't see them even if you saw them, Bheem. They have hooves and hides, fur and antlers, but they are people like you and me. They have mates and children, and all of them came this morning to plead with their beautiful, dumb eyes."

"And what did they plead for?" Bheem asked, scratching, stretching, and yawning.

"Their lives. One of them came and knelt before me. 'Majesty, very few of us remain now,' he said. 'In a short while, our race will be extinct. Please protect us from Bheem.'"

Bheem laughed loudly, as if Yudhishtra was pulling his leg.

"We must move on and let them recover, Bheem."

"Move on? But this is a wonderful place to stay. We have lived here for ten years. The forest fulfills all our needs! Oh my gentle brother, you have to stop assigning your own sensibility to them. They are merely animals."

"No, Bheem. They bleed and die, they feel all the emotions we feel: hunger, tiredness, fear, loss, love. The division between us and them is Maya—illusion, ignorance. How can you not see that they have the same consciousness as we?"

"Except, as you yourself just said, they are dumb."

"They communicate with a faculty deeper than words, in a manner that we humans have forgotten. We think language is the only way. Sometime when I meditate, I am so still that the deer come up to me and lie down beside me. And when this happens I feel the very mystery and magic of the universe has come into my presence. The stillness I attain through constant practice is theirs naturally. If I had to judge, I would say they are superior to us. These gentle creatures live with vigilance, and die in the spirit of sacrifice. When we eat meat, we must be aware with every mouthful how their life sustains us. And now, we must concede to their wish, Bheem. If we don't, we will perpetuate the tragedy that Pandu visited on our family."

It had been a while since anyone mentioned Pandu, the patriarch of the family, and his manner of dying. With his two wives, Kunti and Madri, Pandu had retired to the forest to live the life of a hermit. Once when he was out hunting, he shot an arrow at two deer in the act of mating. The doe died at once, and the grief-stricken and distraught male cursed the king: "the next time you make love to your wife, sire, you will fall down dead!"

For years Pandu refrained from sex with his wives, but one day, seeing Madri emerge still wet from her bath in the river, he was unable to restrain himself. Pandu made love to her, and fell stone dead upon her chest. Yudhishtra had grown up in the shadow of this story, and therefore knew how imperative it was to have an affinity and empathy with animals. He understood with unerring clarity that we share the planet with them and must treat them with affection and kindness.

Bheem was silent for a while, but unconvinced about his brother's point of view. "Well, look at it like this. If Pandu hadn't died, we wouldn't be the sons of gods."

The two brothers sat silently, recalling their history. Before her

marriage to Pandu, Kunti was blessed by a sage: she could summon any god of her choice and conceive a child by him. After Pandu died without producing any children, Kunti availed herself of her boon.

"I am the son of Vayu, Lord of the Winds and of Breath, and you, the son of Dharma, Lord of Moral Law," Bheem said. "Ah, I understand now why you are so fastidiously virtuous, brother."

"Dharma, Bheem, means more than virtue. To live with dharma is to live with a vision of life in which all living things are woven into one seamless and harmonious design. You cannot ignore one part of this web without harming yourself. You are it, and it is you. The whole and the individual are inseparable, brother. Dharma demands we be in tune with nature."

"Ah, nature," Bheem said. "Look at this dead cedar tree, this fallen giant. Look how many insects and plants live upon its crumbling body. Relax, brother, relax. Nature would not have invented death if there wasn't a purpose to it."

"We must stop eating the deer or move on, Bheem."

"Stop eating them? If we are going to fight a war and win, we need to be robust and well nourished. We don't want to become like Mankanaka, that other defender of the animals. He would eat only green leaves, grasses, and fruit!"

"I remember his story now! He was very strong, wasn't he?"

"The point of the story was that one day he cut his finger on a tree limb, and what do you think poured out of him?"

"Glorious green sap! Oh, how happy that made him!"

"Blood is our heritage, brother."

"Alas!"

"No, not alas. Bright red blood is what makes us who and what we are. It is the color and expression of our energy."

"The blood of every living creature is also red."

"And that is why they eat each other."

"Yet Mankanaka was very happy to see the sap. The sight made him dance with joy. And so beautiful and powerful was his dance that everything began to dance along with him: lions, birds, fish, trees, mountains, clouds, rivers, all of them thumping and jostling and . . ."

". . . and veering off course, upsetting the laws of the gods. Even the sun swung in the ecliptic, and the earth rotated wildly on its axis, and the planets and stars flew off their tracks and threatened to destroy the earth."

"They were remaking the world so it would be less brutal. Dancing instead of warring, rejoicing instead of killing. "

"Till the gods summoned Shiva, and said, 'our world is in danger from dancing itself to death. We must stop this madman now. Make him eat meat at once!'"

"No, no," Yudhishtra amended the story. "Nothing was said about eating meat. Shiva stood near Mankanaka. This dance was even more awesome than his own dance at Tillai, the center of the universe. Shiva said to Mankanaka, 'Please stop dancing for a moment and tell me why you dance.' Mankanaka paused . . ."

". . . and the whole world returned mercifully to its familiar and age-old ways. . ."

127

Bheem interrupted.

". . . and Mankanaka showed Shiva his finger," Yudhishtra continued, "from which sap still spurted, drop by green drop. Shiva smiled, and said, 'is that all? Look!' and then Shiva dug the nail of one hand into the veins of his other arm, and ashes white as snow flakes poured out, swirling in the air. Ashes, ashes everywhere—from the heart of our Lord of Ascetics, the King of Control."

"Harrumph!" snorted Bheem. "And I suppose you want to be like Shiva?"

"I wish. But since I am much too human for my liking, I would like at least for us to move on if we can't stop eating the deer, and let them recoup their numbers. We cannot harm animals without harming ourselves. You know why Dhritrashtra was born blind?"

"He's blind because he is stupid and spiritually blind. He has nurtured his sons' evil. I can't wait to kill all his sons and drink their blood."

"No, Bheem. Too much blood in your veins makes you blind to the virtues of our enemies. Let's give Dhritrashtra his due. He keeps his balance between power and kindness, personal preference and justice. He has a deep spiritual side and his lack of sight has given him extraordinary insight. Once he made it a discipline to explore one hundred of his past lives. He can scroll backward in time."

"Can he go forward in time and see how we are going to squash their brains and turn them into meatballs?"

"Your violence, Bheem, is a direct result of your excessive love of meat. Listen to this story, and you may learn something from it. In his journey through his past lives, Dhritrashtra discovered that in all of those one hundred lives he had been a good, law-abiding man. He hadn't harmed others and was always compassionate. He wondered why fate had made him blind and could find no cause in his previous lifetimes that would merit such privation. Once he asked Krishna, 'Lord, please tell me what sin I have committed to be born blind. Is the universe blind, that it punishes innocents for no fault of theirs?'"

"Dhritrashtra, innocent!" Bheem snorted.

"Krishna bade him sit in meditation and look into his past lives, and Dhritrashtra laughed. 'I have already explored one hundred of my past lives and found no cause for it.' But Lord Krishna said, 'go back further still.' Dhritrashtra sat in meditation, and found that once, in a lifetime long ago, he had pierced a thorn in the eyes of an insect and blinded it."

"Oh, mere insects," Bheem said, swatting a big mosquito on his shoulder.

"Brother, you were there when Krishna said: 'we are on the wheel of life, wandering from one birth to the next. Sometimes we are kings, and sometimes we live out our lives on a blade of grass.'"

"But Yudhishtra, do you remember what he said immediately after that? 'But we always live. Nothing can stop that wheel. Consciousness is eternal. Nothing and no one will make us lose that force, whatever happens.' So, my dear brother, sometimes we kill in order to free the souls from their miserable lives on blades of grass," Bheem said, swatting another insect on his arm.

Bheem got up, stretched, reached for his bow and arrow that hung on the tree, and went off to find breakfast.

Yudhishtra watched his brother disappear into the forest, his massive form knocking down vines and branches before him. Yudhishtra then turned and went inside the cottage to talk to his other brothers and wife, to convince them to move on.

At a distance amidst the foliage, the deer people watched, waited, and hoped.

See Him in the Dark

*t*he Pandava brothers were worried about the upcoming war with their cousins, the Kauravas. The latter had exiled the Pandavas to the forest for thirteen years after defeating them in a loaded game of dice, and had taken over their kingdom, the treasury, and the arsenals.

In the forest where they were hiding, the Pandavas met a holy man who told them that one of the brothers needed to go to Mount Kailash, the abode of Shiva, to pray, meditate, and fast in order to obtain a vision of the Beautiful Lord. If he were successful at this, he would acquire the divine bow, Gandiva, and other celestial arms that would help them in the war. But, the holy man warned, whoever was sent on this quest must not allow himself to be distracted from his mission by anything. He would have to be entirely focused on the task at hand.

Their choice fell immediately on Arjuna. Single-minded purpose was Arjuna's strength. His brothers and his cousins had witnessed this trait of Arjuna's from an incident in their youth. They had all trained together in archery and their great instructor, Drona Acharya, had put them to a test. Drona sewed a parrot out of green fabric, attached a red chili for a beak, painted a red and black eye upon it, and perched it high on a treetop. Then he invited all the boys to aim their arrows at the target: the eye of the bird.

Drona called Yudhishtra first to try.

"What do you see?" Drona asked, as Yudhishtra prepared to shoot his arrow.

"I see a blue sky with a few white clouds in it, a tall tree, green leaves, and a stuffed parrot."

"Don't even try," said Drona to Yudhishtra, who lowered the bow and stepped aside.

Drona then called upon the other Pandava brothers and the Kauravas. Asking them the same question—"what do you see?"—he got similar answers. Some of the youths saw the fruit on the tree besides the parrot, some saw Drona from the corners of their eyes in addition to the bird, and some focused on their own hand pulling the string of the bow as they aimed their arrow towards the bird. Drona dismissed each of them before they had a chance to shoot.

When Arjuna stepped forward for his turn, his bow bent and ready, Drona asked him the same question.

"I see the black pupil of the eye rimmed with red," Arjuna replied.

"What kind of a tree is it?" Drona asked.

"I don't know. I see only the eye of the bird."

"What is the color of the bird?" Drona asked.

"I don't know. I see only the eye."

Exhilarated that he had produced if only one student who understood archery, Drona said, "Shoot, Arjuna!" With unwavering aim, Arjuna had shot the bird through its eye.

Though this feat alone earned Arjuna untold respect, over the years he became even more skilled, training himself to target such small and distant objects even in the dark.

So, now, a fully mature man on a mission to behold a vision of Shiva, Arjuna determined not to be deflected by anything he might encounter. He would defeat anyone who opposed him in his quest, overcome temptations, and achieve his aim.

Carrying his bow, his quiver, and his sword, Arjuna climbed the mountain of snow, the abode of Lord Shiva. It was a long, exhausting journey. The sun barely shone as Arjuna climbed in the endless cold, gray light. His attention and energy was focused upon the treacherous climb up the path of icy steps made by the matted roots of trees. At one point, he noticed the roots were made of gold studded with precious gems, but knew that this was a temptation by the gods, so he carried on.

As Arjuna climbed higher, coming around a bend in the way, he saw the dangling, dirty feet of someone sitting on a boulder. He stopped and looked up to see a man in ragged clothes, drinking something out of a clay cup. All around him were trees made of the brightest gold, with leaves made of precious stones. A breeze blowing through them made a delicate music, soothing and restful.

"This," said the old man, "is the Forest of Bliss. Throw away your weapons and live here in peace forever."

"My destination, old man, is Lord Shiva, The Beautiful One, the one with the crescent moon in his hair. I am here to seek celestial weapons, not peace," Arjuna said.

"You're not seeking peace?" the man said. "Man! Peace, shanti, is the endeavor of all humankind!"

"Not mine," said Arjuna. "What is peace to me when the injustice in the world must be fought? When my brothers and kinsmen suffer? Keep your peace, old man."

"Bliss, then. It is a step above peace. Why labor and struggle when you can have bliss?"

"Don't try to tempt me, you won't succeed. I am not about to enter bliss and leave my brothers helpless."

"Have a drink, then," the old man said, extending the cup towards Arjuna.

"That I will do, for I am thirsty."

Arjuna put down his weapons briefly, took the cup and drained it. When he threw it away, it exploded like a thunderbolt. When he looked up, he saw that the old man was none other than Lord Indra.

"Well done, my son," he said slapping Arjuna on the shoulder. "I am very proud of your strength and resolution. Go with my blessing to Lord Shiva, and may you succeed in your quest."

Arjuna carried on, renewed by the drink, and laughing to himself that Indra had been so naive as to think he, Arjuna, would not be able to see through his disguise. How the gods underestimated mortals!

Arjuna came to a grove, a haven of spring where exquisite flowers grew even in the winter. He put aside his weapons, and prepared to fast, pray, and meditate on Shiva.

But first he wanted to string a garland of wild flowers for Shiva. He picked fragrant yellow roses, white jasmine, anemones, irises, peonies, and leaning over precipitous cliffs he plucked violet and red rhododendron blooms. With each flower he strung he recounted one of Shiva's attributes: "Beautiful. Bountiful. Blue Throated. Sky Clad. Adored. Attractive. Alluring. Magnificent. Full of Light. Splendid. Destroyer of Evil. Bestower of Peace. Giver of Ecstasy," and so, on and on, till the garland was knotted and complete.

Then Arjuna made a clay statue of Shiva, and hung the garland around its neck till the time he would see the deity in person. He said a prayer to Shiva, humbly and earnestly beseeching the god not to abandon him in the battlefield of life, to stay close, to instruct him, to help him to discern and be courageous in these difficult times of conflict and impending war.

"Be with me," he supplicated. "Help me choose the right path, your path, the path of light and goodness and love. And please, bestow upon me your celestial weapons."

Then Arjuna sat down to meditate for as long as it took for him to obtain the object of his devotion. In his mind's eye he saw how Shiva would appear to him: resplendent and bright. Then, placing his weapons within reach, he went into a deep trance.

Sometime later, Arjuna heard rustling nearby, and, being a seasoned warrior as well as a consummate archer who could hit his target even in the dark, he instantaneously picked up his bow and arrow and shot in the direction of the sound. A wild boar had broken through the underbrush and was charging towards him. Shot through its heart, it now fell at his feet, dead. Arjuna noticed a strange, mystical silence all around him. He bent down to remove the arrow from the body of the animal when he noticed that two arrows—not one—had pierced the boar through the heart and caused his death. He had shot but a single arrow.

As Arjuna straightened up, two arrows whistled past his ears, grazing them. As he strung his bow again, a huge, fierce looking, dark demon, many times Arjuna's size, appeared before him. He wore a garland of skulls around his neck, and carried a sword dripping with blood. Two sharp, white fangs protruded out of his mouth, also covered with fresh blood.

"Ah, ha!" Arjuna thought. "Another test, another temptation, this time to fear. No, nobody gets the better of me! Not with weapons! Not with the bow and arrow! And as for fear, nobody frightens Arjuna!"

With the speed of lightning, he strung his bow again and again and shot a hundred arrows at the demon, but to his amazement, the demon's body just absorbed all of them as if he was made of air. The creature kept advancing towards Arjuna, waving his sword, roaring with loud sounds that pierced Arjuna's ears with their cacophony. "How dare you shoot at my quarry?" the demon said in a voice like thunder.

"How was I to know it was yours? But now that I have killed him, he is mine."

"'Mine! Mine!' Coward! Is this the best you can do?" The demon blew upon Arjuna, and sent him flying backwards against a tree. Arjuna recovered from his fall, and reached for more arrows, but his quiver, which was supposed to be inexhaustible, was suddenly empty. He grabbed his sword and moved towards the demon, who, with one strike of his sword, sent Arjuna's sword flying through the air.

"I still have my body left," Arjuna said. "If you want to fight fairly, put aside your weapons and wrestle with me." The demon put aside his weapons, and with one wave of his hand, sent Arjuna up in the air like a feather. He somersaulted and then began to fall down to the earth.

"Shiva," Arjuna prayed, as he fell towards the earth like a stone, "help me defeat this ugly, uncouth, evil monster! Send me your strength and courage, for I would kill him who stands in the way of my meditation and prayer, I would destroy anything that keeps me from you. Shiva, help!"

Arjuna landed on a bed of moss, which broke the severity of his fall, and he instantly sprang up to resume his battle. Quick as lightning, he came up with a plan to whiz past the demon and tackle him from behind. But as he ran past him, the demon grabbed him and carried him, struggling and squirming, towards his gory mouth.

Arjuna was awestruck by what he saw. Looking in the monster's mouth he saw fragments of human bones and hide stuck between his teeth, and upon his tongue gouts of blood and hair. Arjuna turned his attention to the demon's eyes and saw that they were cold, impassive, and without mercy. And for the first time in his life, Arjuna felt fear grip his heart. All his prayers to Shiva had gone unheeded.

"Admit you are defeated before I eat you," the demon said to him. "Surrender to me!"

"I am not defeated!" Arjuna said, but his voice was shaking and unconvincing. The demon laughed in his face, and cruel laughter it was, full of derision.

"I am Arjuna, Drona's famous pupil, marksman beyond compare, and nothing will stand in my way."

"Admit defeat," the demon repeated. "Surrender."

"I admit you are as good a marksman as I am. I bow to your superior ability and strength. Now put me down and let us have another bout of wrestling," Arjuna said, stalling for time.

"You think you stand a chance of defeating me, you paltry mortal?" the demon said.

"I am certain," Arjuna said.

"Certain?" The demon squeezed Arjuna, and he felt the wind taken out of him by the powerful hand that held him in the air.

For the first time in his life, Arjuna began to weep uncontrollably. He felt as helpless as a child, and knew in his heart that unless Shiva worked a miracle, his life was about to end. He cried at the thought of all his brothers and his wife who would wait in vain for him to return with his celestial weapons. But he still hoped Shiva would rescue him.

"Give up all hope!" the demon said, reading his thoughts. The demon tightened his grip, and Arjuna's entire life flashed before his eyes. As his head swirled in a free fall into a dark and starless abyss, his tongue repeated over and over, "Shiva, save me! Save me, Shiva!" Then he passed out in the demon's hand.

Arjuna came to, his entire body aching and broken in his battle with the demon who, for some reason, had not eaten him. He opened an eye and saw blearily through it that he lay before the clay statue of Shiva that he himself had made. "Thank you for rescuing me," he thought, with a brain that felt like it had been bashed into a pulp. "Thank you."

When Arjuna opened his other eye, and could focus better, he saw that the garland he had strung and put around the statue's neck was missing. He looked around, and saw in the distance that the demon that had almost devoured him was still there, sitting on a boulder, staring at him. Arjuna felt fear return, but when he saw that the demon had removed the garland from the statue and was wearing it around his neck, a fierce anger arose in him. Arjuna rose unsteadily on his feet and lurched towards the demon.

"That," he said as he tottered towards him, "you can't have! That is a symbol of my devotion and respect for Shiva, the Beautiful God, my Lord of Love and Light."

"I also want your devotion and respect," the demon said.

"The garland is for Shiva alone. I don't care how little life is left in me. I will fight you with whatever I have to get it back. I haven't given up hope that Shiva will come for this garland before I die."

"I've defeated you," said the demon, "and you and everything you own now belongs to me, including this garland. Admit defeat."

"I admit defeat only to Shiva," Arjuna said, amazed that the demon did not resist him when he reached towards him and took off the garland. He staggered towards the statue and placed the garland around it once more.

"Shiva, accept this, my last offering to you," Arjuna said, as he broke down before it and wept. When he lifted his head up and wiped his tears, he saw that the garland was gone again. He looked back and saw that it was around the demon's neck again.

"Stop taking away my last gift to Shiva with your evil arts!" Arjuna scolded, and removing the garland once more, strung it around the neck of the statue. But again the garland disappeared.

Arjuna walked towards the demon again, but this time his brain cleared and he realized in an instant who the demon was.

"Shiva!" he said, and fell down at his feet, sobbing and bathing them with his tears. "Forgive me! Forgive my blindness! How could I have not recognized you, Lord? I admit defeat. I have been blind. I surrender. I surrender. I surrender, Shiva!"

And when he was done weeping, he raised his eyes and Shiva was back in his familiar form, a shimmering sliver of moon in his hair, the river cascading down from his head, his eyes like lotuses, his throat blue like the iridescent wings of a butterfly.

"But how could . . . how did you . . . what form . . . ?" Arjuna stammered, unable to comprehend how his beloved Shiva could assume such an evil and ugly countenance.

"You have a very partial image of me in your head, young warrior. You have to recognize me in all that exists—including what seems to you to be ugly and evil. See me in the dark, Arjuna, in that which you cannot defeat and which your human will cannot conquer. See me in misfortune. See me in the downtrodden, the wounded, and the defeated. Remember these words as you go into battle."

Shiva produced Gandiva, the divine bow, and gave it to Arjuna. "Use it only as a last resort, after all efforts at conciliation have failed. Do not use this awesome weapon against the feeble, the innocent, and the weak. And remember, only the humble can use it well."

"But how can I accept Gandiva when I have failed . . ."

Shiva laughed. "See me even in failure, Arjuna. Know that sometimes admitting defeat, within or without, can also be a sign of success."

You

each of the clashing sides, the Pandavas and Kauravas, was getting ready for the war. Each was amassing weapons, building
up armies, and acquiring allies. Though the opponents were family—
blood-cousins, in fact—they had let their discord bring them to the
battlefield.

Both the warring parties decided independently to try to win their
cousin, Krishna, over to their side. The Kauravas sent Duryodhana, and
the Pandavas, Arjuna.

For his part, Duryodhana didn't truly believe, as the Pandavas did,
that Krishna was a god. His main motive was to secure for his own side
Krishna's army of a hundred thousand well-trained men. Duryodhana
was certain that there was no one he could not defeat, if only he had
proper weapons and armies. He was eager to defeat the Pandavas, to
destroy their very seed.

Duryodhana nurtured a long list of grievances against his cousins.
He insisted the royal throne of Hastinapur was rightfully his, despite
the fact that the Pandava's father, Pandu, had been crowned king.
Duryodhana argued that the only reason Pandu was king was because
his own father, who was the older brother, was blind. He was convinced the throne was his because he was the eldest son of the older of
the two brothers, Dhritrashtra.

While his cousins, the Pandavas, felt they ought to have some share
of the kingdom, Duryodhana had refused. He was not ready to share
his power or his wealth. These he considered not only essential, but the

only realities that mattered in life.

In contrast, the Pandavas were what most civilized human beings would consider virtuous. The brothers were fair, polite, reasonable, and noble. Yudhishtra meditated and was a yogi at heart. He was too innocent to realize that the game of dice which he lost, and with it his kingdom, was loaded. Such an unsuspecting, trusting man, Duryodhana believed, would not make a good king. Indeed, the Pandavas' "nobility" really annoyed Duryodhana. He himself had passions and desires which he had no intention of transcending. He liked who he was, and was profoundly annoyed by anyone who suggested by word or deed that he be otherwise. Nature had intended for him to be a particular way. Just as snakes were meant to bite, lions to attack and kill, water to move downhill, and breezes to blow, he, Duryodhana, was what he was. He ridiculed the gods who faulted mortals for behaving as they were created to behave.

Duryodhana called for his fastest chariots and traveled in all haste, through the night, to Dwarka, where Krishna lived. Duryodhana's aim was to preempt Krishna's large and well-quipped army. If he played his cards right, he would make his case to Krishna, who was, above all, reasonable, and would succeed in securing the army long before Arjuna even got there. There was no time to be lost.

Meanwhile, Arjuna, so joyful at the prospect of seeing Krishna again, nearly forgot the purpose of his visit. When he was in Krishna's presence, he was home. Time stood still in the eternal moment where their love breathed its endless song. Waves of joy passed over his heart, spreading their nectar to every particle of his being as he proceeded towards Krishna. And though he traveled alone and had longer to travel, Arjuna arrived there swiftly, on the wings of his heart.

Eager to get there before his cousin, Duryodhana whipped his horses into a frenzy and so arrived in Dwarka first. Sweating and panting, he jumped off his chariot, rushed into Krishna's palace, and headed in the direction of his bedroom. Day had not yet dawned, and Krishna was certain still to be in bed.

Just as he reached Krishna's bedroom door, Duryodhana's mind lurched in disappointment. From the opposite direction, Arjuna was approaching. When Arjuna reached the door a trifle before him, Duryodhana's anger flared. But Arjuna opened the door, and then stood aside calmly and cheerfully, gesturing to Duryodhana to enter first.

Duryodhana felt quashed. The gesture signified everything he disliked about the Pandavas: their smug politeness, their condescending superiority. It reminded him of the time when he had been imprisoned in an iron net by the Gandharvas, Indra's musicians. The Pandavas had found him hanging ignominiously from a tree. They had cut him down, and set him free! And this, after he had usurped his cousins' kingdom, tried to burn, poison, and drown them, exiled them, and insulted their common wife. In fact, Duryodhana had been so humiliated that he had been ready to kill himself over the incident.

Now he had the urge to strike Arjuna, but decided that it was to his advantage to enter the room first. "Fool!" he thought, entering Krishna's bedroom before Arjuna. "This is going to cost you the war! Krishna will now give me first choice, and you are doomed!"

Once inside the bedroom, however, Duryodhana was disappointed to find Krishna still asleep, and so incapable of noticing which cousin entered first. "I will just have to tell him when he awakens," he thought. Duryodhana considered quickly where to sit while he waited for Krishna to awaken. Two chairs stood in the bedroom, one near Krishna's head, the other by his feet. "I should probably take the chair nearest his head, for that is the preeminent position," Duryodhana thought, remembering that Brahmans, India's priestly class, were said to be born

from Brahma's head, while the untouchables sprang from his feet. "But what if . . ."

Before Duryodhana could finish his strategizing, Arjuna, who had followed him in, walked to the foot of the bed, and remained there. Arjuna had no need to deliberate, for his heart carried him to the place from where he could see Krishna sleeping, his beautiful feet peeping from under the silk sheet, like lotuses. Arjuna longed to kiss them but feared awakening Krishna, and refrained. As he gazed at Krishna, beatific and innocent in slumber, tears came to Arjuna's eyes. How long it had been since he had beheld his Lord's dear, dear face! Only a month, but that month felt like an eternity. Arjuna gazed at Krishna long and deep. All the energy and beauty of the universe lay before him on that bed.

Duryodhana, relieved again that Arjuna had made the foolish choice, slid into the chair by the head of the bed, and waited.

It was not long before Krishna awakened and Arjuna felt the entire universe awakened with him. The blue whistling thrush sang its liquid lyric in ascending notes, the first light touched the trees, the dark sky turned blue, and color returned to the world.

The first person Krishna saw upon awakening was Arjuna leaning against the bed post, looking upon him with love-filled eyes. Krishna's face lit up with a smile at the sight before him. Arjuna! Dear friend, beloved devotee! He embraced him with his eyes as he stretched.

From his post beside the bed, Duryodhana saw the look in Arjuna's eyes, and knew at once that Krishna was awake. He jumped up from the chair. "I entered the room first!" he cried out quickly.

"But I saw Arjuna first," Krishna said. "Speak, Arjuna, why have you come? What can I do for you?"

Duryodhana fumed inwardly. This was unfair! This was favoritism! Arjuna would ask for Krishna's army, he knew, and all his effort would have been in vain!

But Arjuna looked at Krishna, forgot what he came for, and remained silent.

"Know, Pandava, that I am not going to take any sides in the war. I will not fight personally, not carry a weapon, but I can act as a moral guide. So you can have either my army of a hundred thousand, or you can have me," Krishna said, sitting up in bed. "Speak, Arjuna."

Without any hesitation, Arjuna said, "You." Then he fell at Krishna's feet, and kissed them.

Duryodhana felt elated. "Stupid fool!" he reveled inwardly. "You choose moral guidance over a hundred thousand warriors fighting for you with the best weapons! But why should I complain about your folly when it serves me well? Moral guidance, ha!"

Before Krishna even turned towards Duryodhana, the latter burst out, "The army! I'll take the army, then!"

"It is yours, Duryodhana."

Happy at acquiring his heart's desire, ebullient at his palpable, quantitative success, Duryodhana bowed before Krishna, and hurried out to inspect the army and make preparations to take them with him to his headquarters.

How the war between the two families progressed, and how it concluded is another long story. Because he had the arsenal and the manpower, Duryodhana was certain of victory. Arjuna had just Krishna, who was not going to fight or wield a weapon.

"Be my charioteer in the battlefield, Lord," Arjuna asked. "Speak to me in a voice that is clear and unhampered by doubt. Guide me; help me think the right thought, make the right move. Teach me how to think, what to think. I ask for nothing else." Krishna nodded his head, and Arjuna was filled with confidence and joy.

So it was that when, at the beginning of the war, Arjuna despaired at the fratricidal war, doubted his own adequacy, and feared for the lives of those he loved, Krishna sang to him the Song of God, which dispelled his doubts and his sorrow, filled him with courage to do the righteous deed regardless of outcome and consequence, and infused him with fearlessness in the face of death by giving him a vision of his own deathless and eternal soul.

With Krishna's constant guidance, the Pandavas fought fearlessly. Though their numbers were far, far fewer than those of the Kauravas, they won. How could they not? Krishna had taught them the most fundamental of truths—that it is consciousness that creates reality.

THE BIRD WHO
FOUGHT WAR

*t*he armies of both sides, the Pandavas and the Kauravas, were
mobilized and ready. Horses snorted and neighed, elephants
trumpeted, conch shells resounded in the air, war drums rolled. The
Mahabharata, the Great War between good and evil, was about
to begin.

Krishna, sitting alongside Arjuna in his glorious chariot drawn by
white horses, drew an arrow from his quiver, strung it on his mighty
bow, and was about to let it fly—a signal that the war had begun—
when Chidia, a little bird, flew into his line of vision, and perched
herself on the yoke of the horses. Looking as aggressive and intimidat-
ing as she could, her feathers fluffed up in anger, she looked at Krishna
and Arjuna and declared:

"I will not let this war proceed."

The young soldiers standing by, eager, ready, and chafing at the bit
for battle, laughed in disbelief and derision. Krishna and Arjuna, momentarily distracted from the tremendous task ahead of them, looked at
each other and smiled.

"Oh?" said Arjuna. "Are you, like me, afraid of bloodshed, little
bird? Then let me tell you what wisdom I have just learned from Lord
Krishna here."

"You are the great Lord of the Universe?" said Chidia, turning to

Krishna. "Then you are just the person I wanted to see. My nest is over there on the ground in the fecund, worm-filled grasses beneath that flowering Gulmohar tree. My five fledglings hatched a few days ago. I cannot have elephants and horses, chariots and crazed men trampling the fields. You must stop this war immediately. "

The soldiers guffawed and came over to shoo the stupid little bird away, but Krishna held up his hand and stopped the soldiers.

"What kind of a lord are you? Encouraging grown and conscious men to kill each other? Destroying the nests of helpless little birds like me? Annihilating seeds even as they sprout in the earth? Allowing blood to splatter on blossoms, and letting this horrible tumult overpower birdsong?"

While Krishna was thoughtful and silent, Arjuna compassionately continued his dialogue with the bird. It was important to him that the wisdom he had just acquired from Krishna be communicated to even the tiniest creatures of the earth.

"I, too, was distraught and despairing at the thought of killing my brothers and mentors. 'O day of darkness,' I cried. 'What evil spirit moved our minds for the sake of an earthly kingdom to kill our own people?'"

"Exactly," said Chidia. "War is a terrible thing. Let no wisdom from this lord here or anyone else allay that despair."

"Nothing can," Arjuna said, sadly.

"Good," she said, turning to Krishna. "So let's stop this madness right now and the soldiers of both sides return to their peaceful, comfortable nests, delight in children, eat bread made from the grains in their fields, adorn themselves with spring flowers, and make sweet music."

"But neither should we be deterred from the righteous act by fear or cowardice," Arjuna countered. "This is a necessary and important war, and it cannot be put off. Good must fight evil whenever it rears its ugly head."

"I know nothing of righteous acts, of good and evil. I know only that my fledglings have just hatched and that my mate, Chida, and I were very happy till this chaos began. Krishna, do you hear me? Are you deaf? Please, please take your important and righteous war somewhere else, for I won't let you make it here."

"Little bird, everything that is born must die," Arjuna said. "But the spirit is beyond destruction. You, I, your fledglings, my children and brothers and relatives and enemies have all existed for all time. Never was there a time when we weren't, and never will there be a time when we won't be. In the scale of the universe, blood and blossoms, singing and dying, are one. So face what must be, and cease from sorrow."

"Oh," cried Chidia, looking past Arjuna to Krishna, and pleading. "Let not the thread of my song and the song of my children be cut while we sing. Let not my work end before its fulfillment. Let not my happiness be nipped in the bud!"

"We may only accept the ways of the world, little bird," Arjuna said.

"But these are the ways of foolish and ignorant men!" argued Chidia.

"The ways of men, too, are the ways of the world. That which cannot be changed, that which is, is destiny. We can only submit humbly, little being. We can only eat that which is given."

There was a long silence, a wide and ominous calm. Nothing moved, nothing stirred. Chidia suddenly and quietly felt very small. She understood that she was just a tiny, helpless creature who couldn't change the course of history or the huge world in which she lived and bred and sang. Her only recourse was to accept the inevitable war. She lowered her head humbly, and bowed to Krishna.

"I will eat what you give me, if that is the only thing I can do," she said quietly, resignedly. But a moment later, emotion welled up in her, overcoming her wisdom, and she cried, "But, Krishna, Krishna make it sweet, do you hear? And you who hold the universe in your mouth, you who accomplish your purposes through death and destruction, you from whose flute all birds have learnt their song, protect me and mine from this madness, Krishna!" Having said what she came to say, Chidia turned around and flew away.

The young soldiers were glad to see the end of her. Now the action could begin. Arjuna sounded loud his war cry like the roar of the lion, and blew his far-sounding conch shell, which resounded across the field to where the enemy ranks assembled, thousands of warriors in file as far as the eye could see. War drums rumbled, cymbals clashed, trumpets blew and filled the sky with a thunder so fearful that heaven and earth and the hearts of all the soldiers trembled.

Krishna took up his bow again, strung an arrow, and took aim. With a loud twang he let the feathered arrow fly towards the enemy camp.

The surprised soldiers gasped—it seemed that Krishna had faltered and missed the mark. Instead of hitting the enemy's general, or even

the elephant on which he sat, ready to charge, the arrow merely severed
the huge and heavy brass bell around the elephant's neck. It fell to the
ground with a mighty clang.

The war began. And a terrible war it was, sad to see. Eighteen long
days the battle raged. When it was all over, corpses littered the field,
and the earth was soaked with blood. Even the nests on the trees were
knocked to the ground with lances and spears and trampled underfoot
by soldiers, horses, elephants, and chariots.

Krishna, with Arjuna by his side, alighted from his chariot and
walked slowly to the Gulmohar tree. He bent his knees and with
both hands, lifted the elephant's brass bell where it lay on the grasses.
Beneath it Arjuna saw something stirring in the still grasses, and then
with a whirring, whirling sound of delicate wings, five fledglings and
their parents flew, singing, into the blue beyond.

BLIND HUNGER

On her way to the funeral of her one hundred sons—all of them slaughtered in the Great War—Gandhari, mother of the Kauravas, felt her own life was over. There was no way she was going to survive this calamity. She would have to have a heart of stone. Gandhari was a woman who had lived essentially for her husband, Dhritrashtra, and her sons. And now, this. It was too great a grief to bear. She was going to throw herself on the mass pyre and perish. Life was a brutal, miserable thing, and she had had enough of it.

Though Gandhari had been warned against visiting the battlefield, nothing could have prepared her for the ghastly sight before her. Entire acres were strewn with human and animal limbs, bodies, heads, and torsos. And each of these in turn was broken, crushed, rotting. Blood and guts saturated the earth, and the jackals were already feasting to their heart's content. Vultures too partook of the carnage, carrying entrails and large chunks of bone and flesh in their beaks to their nests in the trees, to feed their young.

Gandhari made her way through the stench and sight of putrid and burning human flesh, disembodied parts, to where the body of her favorite son, Duryodhana, lay. Starting from his thigh, his entire body was ripped open to the bone, and his skeleton, also broken and smashed, was visible, ivory beneath the pink of his flesh. His face that she had loved so much was a red splatter of hair and skin, unrecognizable save for one amber eye, which remained open and staring into the sun. Dusasana, her second favorite son, lay close by, with maggots in the mouth she had so often fed from her breast and her hands. The bodies of her other sons too lay helter-skelter all around her.

Her heart felt like it had turned to granite. Nothing stirred inside or outside of her. Just a few rats, who had been partaking of the banquet, their sharp teeth dripping with blood, scurried here and there, tugging at organs.

Suddenly the seeds of rage stirred in Gandhari and she screamed at a rat: "Get away, you foul and heartless animal!" And she lunged at him, falling over bodies herself, but unable to catch him. He simply scuttled away to another body, looked at her impassively, and resumed his eating.

Looking up, Gandhari saw startled to see Lord Krishna approaching, the iridescent peacock feathers in his hair bobbing jauntily in the air. His yellow silk clothes, despite the carnage all around him, were unruffled and clean, his step light and carefree, the garland of wild flowers around his neck ever fresh and undying. He was unmoved by the horror before him. Seeing this, Gandhari's heart leapt with rage, like a flame flaring from a funeral pyre.

"So, Lord of the Universe, you have come, have you, to see your handiwork and rejoice at the slaughter of my sons? Oh you cruel and heartless beast . . ." Gandhari fell upon him like a tigress, beating her fists against his great chest.

"Are you happy now, you, Prime Mover, the Lord responsible for all this? What kind of a god are you who would allow this to happen? You are not a god, but a demon who feasts on hearts, you rat, you vulture, you . . ." And Gandhari let forth a string of abuses so foul that some of the dying opened their eyes momentarily.

Krishna stood calm and silent, absorbing all her curses, for he always viewed everything from the eye of eternity. He saw in its entirety the great, timeless drama that had unfolded out of the fabric of space-time to enfold back into it, leaving a great book behind that would forever entertain and instruct humankind, and show in the mirror of its pages the great face of its formless soul.

Gandhari's rage was spent. For even the greatest of our griefs, like the tides of the ocean, have their limits from which they return to calm. And in the very heart of this stillness Gandhari felt a fierce, insatiable hunger arising. It had been days since she had eaten, her grief having subdued all her natural appetites. It grew now, vast and irrepressible in its urge.

Gandhari cast her eyes about. On a cliff nearby, she spied a bush. Succulent, blood-red berries hung from it in bunches. Over the bodies she stepped, her entire consciousness focused only on the fruit. But when she reached the side of the cliff, the berries were too high up and beyond her reach.

Gathering everything and anything she could, Gandhari made a little mound and climbed upon it. Yes, that worked. She plucked and ate the berries, her taste buds delighting in their luscious flavor, red juice dribbling down her chin. Only when she had eaten her fill of them, and was preparing to climb down the heap of debris, did she notice that she had piled up the bodies of her sons, including Duryodhana's mighty frame of bones, and was standing upon them to quell her own hunger.

ELSEWHERE BOUND

*t*hirty-six years had passed since Yudhishtra, the eldest of the Pandava brothers, had regained the kingdom of Hastinapur, after a long and difficult exile and war. In that time, he became famous throughout India for being one of the greatest kings in history. He was just, upright, magnanimous, peace-loving, and compassionate. Yudhishtra's subjects had grown prosperous and content under his reign. Even nature seemed to be his ally, for the seasonal rains never failed the crops, and not a single natural calamity occurred. The region's wild animals enjoyed all they required of sustenance. Yudhishtra preferred diplomacy and reconciliation with his neighboring kings and kingdoms rather than attempts to subjugate or conquer them, so peace reigned.

The king's greatness had been cultivated over decades. Even as a youth he knew he had to evolve for himself a code of ethics that would ensure the greatest good for him and for all. He chose to live with the faith that all of life—mineral, plant, animal, human—was the manifestation of the One consciousness, related and interrelated intimately. He extended his knowledge of the physical world to his spiritual life as well. Oneness prevailed here, too, connecting pleasure and pain, hope and despair, good and bad fortune. Yudhishtra remained calm and in good spirits through much travail, knowing that there was no tragedy that was not somehow part of the Design. Man was but a pattern in it, a bright arc between two darknesses.

But after thirty-six years of ruling nobly, a weariness that he couldn't shake off took root in his heart. Age weakened Yudhishtra's control upon his psyche, and memories of the terrible war kept floating unbidden into his mind. The cost of victory had taken away its glory, rendering it akin to defeat for him. He and his Pandava brothers had to kill their cousins and uncles, nephews and mentors to win the throne that was rightfully theirs, but now the passing years had smudged the line between success and failure, right and wrong. He wondered whether he should relinquish his throne and take sanyaas, retire to the forest and live like a hermit, but he was unable to accept this idea or any of the other plans he hatched to keep himself going.

As he sat upon his throne one day in an empty hall, Yudhishtra recalled a story that Vyasa, the poet, had told Dhritrashtra, the former king, as he sat upon this very throne. Exhausted with inner turmoil and the tragedy woven into the fabric of life, Dhritrashtra had begged Vyasa to tell him a story.

Vyasa, whose vision transcended the up-and-down revolution of the wheel of life, had complied:

"Listen, Majesty. On a forested island there once lived a man who, from the moment he was born, was in danger of losing his life. He had to do everything just to survive. He tried to escape, but on all sides the island was girded with ferocious and hungry sharks waiting to devour him. In the forest, wild tigers and bears stalked him at every moment. Running away from them, he fell into a deep pit covered by thick vines. As he fell, his foot caught in the matted roots of a tree. And so he hung there, swinging from his heels.

"Beneath him in the dark and unseen depths of the chasm stirred a serpent, waiting eagerly for his prey. Every once in a while he leaped up and bit the hanging man on his head, infusing his poison into his blood. Meanwhile, above the man, a mad elephant, whose every step caused a violent tremor, walked around the rim of the hole. Black and white rats had nearly eaten through the roots that supported him, and the tree hovered precariously over him.

"In the branches of this tree was a bee hive from which dripped, drop by drop, honey on the man's face. He stuck out his tongue and tasted it, always unsatisfied, always wanting more."

Vyasa paused here, to let the symbol sink in. But Dhritrashtra, his hands on his knees as he leaned forward eagerly to hear the end of the story, said, "And?"

"That's all, Majesty."

"That's all?" Dhritrashtra said angrily. "That's all! How can you tell me a story that you don't conclude?"

"It is the story of humankind, Majesty. Such is our life. Calamities and conflict surround and stalk us from our birth, but we cannot get free of our enmeshment because the honey keeps us hooked. Our senses lead us, and we want more and more and more."

"I am done with the honey and the poison," Yudhishtra thought, getting off the throne, and limping to the window. His joints had begun to bother him. The wounds he had suffered in the war had developed tongues and were moaning. "My tongue has tasted all there is to taste on this planet, and more. My eyes and ears have seen and heard enough of the terror and beauty of life. One thing alone remains: to die."

Yudhishtra was reconciled to the inevitability of his death. It was his constant awareness of the certainty of death that had facilitated the flowering of his character into the very acme of humanhood. Because he knew his life was transient, he lived it lightly, with great detachment and compassion.

Now, as he stood before the window, his hands wide open by his side, he not merely accepted the human destiny of death, but actively said "yes" to it. A longing arose in him for reunion with that eternity and unity from which he had been thrust into duration and conflict at birth. He wanted to go to that home which no one could take away from him, which did not need to be constantly defended, and rest.

In the distance, he saw the gardens of his palace, and the other magnificent buildings in which lived his brothers and his wife. The interconnected web of his relationships with them had brought much solace in the past. He had struggled and sometimes fought with them, but always in the context of connection and love. His engagement in family matters was a result of his conviction that family was the battlefield in which, by defeating the demon of ego, one learned the essential lessons of living and loving.

But now Yudhishtra's love of family had attenuated, thinned. Weariness did what all his wisdom could not do earlier: dissolve his attachments to the members of his family for whose happiness and welfare he had lived. He had juggled their five voices in his head, fought a war to win a kingdom for them, and become royal sovereign on their behalf. He was not a warrior at heart, like his other brothers, Arjuna and Bheem. Left to himself, he would have been a yogi, meditating and observing with awe and wonder his inner processes and the ways of the world.

He called his brothers—Bheem, Arjuna, Nakula, Sahdeva—and their wife, Draupadi, and told them about his intent. There were no protests from them. They huddled together in a corner of the hall, and after a brief conference, stood before him to tell him about their own unfaltering pledge to accompany him to Mt. Meru, center of the universe, from which all life comes, and to which it ineluctably and unerringly returns. Having acted out the tragic melodrama of life, they were ready to let it all go. Their epic was over, and only the last act remained.

The entourage's departure did not take long, for in this final journey, there is nothing to take, but only to give away and let go. Yudhishtra called Parakshit, Arjun's grandson, and bequeathed the kingdom to him. Draupadi gave away her clothes and jewels, Sahdeva his many books, and Nakula his collection of silver and gold mirrors.

Leaving behind Hastinapur's fortifications and palaces, which had protected and imprisoned them, they stepped out of the gate, where the throngs wept and bewailed their loss. Many of them wanted to follow the Pandavas in their journey, but Yudhishtra forbade them. He was unable, however, to dissuade a small black dog with spiked white hair on his muzzle that attached himself to the party and would not leave. They tried to shoo him away, but with his perked ears cocked to one side, his silken tail wagging, he looked at them so plaintively with his dark eyes that Draupadi picked him up in her arms.

"Oh, let us take him with us for a short while."

Yudhishtra was too preoccupied to resist, so the dog followed them all the way to the sea, where Arjuna and Bheem prepared to consign their weapons to the waters. The mighty, fearless, and fallible Bheem, whose passionate purpose had been to stoke within himself something of the dark energy necessary to combat the forces of evil and greed, swung his club for the last time. After a loud but brief splash it sunk silently to the bottom. Arjuna placed his mighty bow upon the sands and arranged his quiver, shield, and swords upon it as if it were a boat, then launched it on the waters. It bobbed up and down on the surf, and when it was past the breakers in the broad, wide sea, it somehow caught the wind and, like a ship in a gale, flew into the darkness beyond.

It was the surrender of their weapons that brought home to all of them the finality of their end. After a lifetime aimed at survival, it was time now to move consciously towards that very event that they had spent their entire lives avoiding and defeating.

And so, defenseless as when they first entered life, and totally at the mercy of the matrix that birthed them and to which they were now returning, they set forth again, the dog still at their heels, on the final leg of their journey, Yudhishtra leading the way. They didn't talk, for all words were spent. In this hiatus between life and death, each relived a lifetime compressed into a few moments that stood out from the darkness like lighted tableaus.

The landscape in which they moved became gradually unfamiliar, birthed into and accustomed as they were to form, color, lines, and boundaries. The world as they knew it appeared to be melting back into the plasma from which it had emerged. Nothing was distinct and certain any more. The sun, Lord of Life, which had made eyes and the mind, and had given objects for them to play upon, now turned unfamiliar: dark, and also unbearably bright, at once cold and scorching. At the gateway of the infinite, all contraries coalesced. No shadows and shades, no breeze or wind touched the Pandavas—echoes between two sounds, words dissolving into silence, star shine of suns no longer in existence—as they trudged up the slope of the mountain of jagged grey rock towards the event horizon, the point of infinity where all matter condenses back to formless energy.

One by one their bodies fell. Draupadi collapsed first into a lifeless heap. The dog licked her face, moaned softly, and then followed the others. Then Arjuna, Sahdeva, Nakula, and finally Bheem fell.

In the twilight between life and death, Yudhishtra cared deeply and felt nothing at all. With his resolve he had severed all his attachments of the heart. Now he didn't sigh or look back. Consciously, he was too wise to grieve for what must be. He carried on alone. Only the dog still followed him.

"Go away, dog. Don't follow me. I am elsewhere bound and will not keep you company much longer."

But the dog had no ears for words, and persisted in following him. He played around the king's heels, jumped upon him, and licked his hands. Gentle Yudhishtra, once so attached to earth's creatures, couldn't help but reach out and stroke him. "You follow me at your own peril, little puppy. Don't get attached to me, for nothing is going to keep me from moving on."

The dog bounded ahead, leaping upon the rough and irregular grey cliffs and boulders. Every once in a while the dog peered over the cliff, ears cocked, head to one side, bright eyed, keenly looking to make sure his adopted owner was well, and following him.

For the first time since his journey began, Yudhishtra's heart stirred with old, mortal feelings. He felt grateful to this animal for looking out for him. "But," he told himself. "No attachment. I haven't given up all the accouterments of life only to leash myself to a dog."

His resolution held till he discovered that the dog, who had now been following him, was nowhere to be seen. "Just as well," Yudhishtra told himself. "He has finally decided to return to his real master, wherever he is. What would I, bound for eternity, have done with him, anyway? There are, as far as I know, no dogs in heaven."

As Yudhishtra continued to climb, he recalled how Brahmans considered dogs unclean animals. They had fleas and ticks, mites and dander, and their ubiquitous hair always flew into food or the prayer bowl full of flowers and offerings. Dogs also loved to roll on dung, and who knew where their paws and tongues had been? Yudhishtra himself belonged to the warrior class, and had no such qualms. He loved animals, but it was just as well that the dog had returned to his owner.

As Yudhishtra proceeded, the thought entered his mind that perhaps the dog was injured. He had never abandoned one in need, or one who was too weak to protect himself. Despite his rapidly dimming hearing, he thought he heard a high-pitched whine. It was a king's duty to protect any being that came within his ambit. Yudhishtra turned around and went back to the place where he had last seen the dog. Though exhausted from lack of food and the strenuousness of his journey, he called out, "Puppy! Puppy! Boy! Where are you?"

He cupped his ears to hear better, but was not hopeful of finding the animal. The dog was surefooted and agile, and it was unlikely that he had fallen off a cliff, Yudhishtra reasoned. "Just as well," he repeated to himself again, and turned to go. Once more he thought he heard a whimpering. Yudhishtra leaned over the cliff, and there was the dog, perched precariously on a narrow ledge. He had, indeed, fallen. Cowering, he looked up at Yudhishtra piteously.

Though the climb down was treacherous, Yudhishtra went to fetch him. What was there to fear when one was journeying to meet Lord Death himself? Vultures were wheeling overhead and the dog needed rescuing. Carefully he succeeded in getting a foothold on the ledge. The dog wagged his tail and tenderly licked his hand in gratitude. Yudhishtra picked him up, and placed him on the footpath above. Then he himself climbed back up on the path to join the dog.

Looking at him, Yudhishtra admitted to himself that he felt a flood of relief. His heart opened in affection for the animal, and in gratitude to the universe for reuniting them. He would not have been able to die in peace if he had shirked his responsibility in trying to find him.

Yudhishtra sat down, and petted the dog, tenderness pouring out of the nerves in his palms. He allowed the animal to lick his face and neck, permited himself to feel, once again, all the sweetness of attachment. This feeling reached beyond his need to protect and defend this dependent animal. He was bound in a manner more primal than he had experienced with his brothers and wife—perhaps because they could speak, and speech was always ambiguous and flawed by the ego's battle to protect itself. But with this *baizubaan janwar*, this wordless animal, there was no social armoring or pretense. "I am glad I found you again. Come on, let us carry on. The future will take care of itself when it becomes the Now."

They came upon a plateau where their climb ended. There was nowhere else to go. A grey and nebulous space surrounded them. As Yudhishtra wondered where there was to go from here, celestial music wafted to his ears. Something whirled in the air. He looked up and saw the bottom of an aerial chariot hovering over him.

"Yudhishtra!" said a voice from within the music. "King amongst men, you have made it to heaven! Because of your nobility, your upright, resolute nature, and your compassion, you are allowed to enter paradise in your body!" The chariot landed and Indra stepped out. In the chariot with him was Yama, Lord of the Dead, come to welcome Yudhishtra to Vaikunth, land of the gods. Behind them played the gandharvas, divine musicians with instruments never heard on earth.

"Step in! Step in!" Lord Yama said.

On the verge of entering paradise, Yudhishtra felt sorrow arise in his heart as he looked down from his height and saw the bodies of his brothers and his wife, like little dots on the scorching and frigid grey sands below. He allowed himself the emotions that had ebbed in the travail of his journey: Never to see them again! Never, dear heaven, to hear their voices! Never to quarrel with them! All his wisdom dissolved, and Yudhishtra allowed himself to weep. Tears streaming down his face, he turned to Indra, folded his hands, and said:

"Lord, if I have truly merited heaven, grant in your mercy that my brothers and wife accompany me."

"Their spirits are already there!" Indra said.

Yudhishtra wiped his tears, and smiled. Relieved that he had arrived at the end of his journey and could now rest, Yudhishtra stepped aside to let his devoted hound precede him into the chariot.

"No, no," said Indra. "You have earned this by your dharma. Not the dog."

The dog whined.

"Without the dog? He has followed me loyally, kept me company in my desolation, and offered affection when I most needed it. I cannot abandon him now. I pray, please let him come with me."

"This can never be, King Yudhishtra. You have come all this way, and the dog is a small thing compared to the joys of heaven. Come, come, and enter."

"Lord Indra, even in heaven, how could I be content if I desert this creature now? He will haunt me forever. Look at him."

The dog wagged his tail as Indra looked at him. With a small yelp, Indra fell backwards as the dog jumped on him in his bid to lick his cheeks. "Down, you filthy creature!" Indra screamed. "Heaven will be defiled by your presence. Come on, make haste, king, let's be off."

Yudhishtra planted his feet firmly, and said, "No."

"You are refusing heaven because of a dog? Can it be that the great, wise king, who has given up his empire, is now attached to this thing with no soul? "

"Forgive me, but everything has a soul, Lord Indra. I would rather give up heaven than this conviction. I will not betray the trust that this small being has placed in me."

"You're mad," Indra said. "But it is your own decision. The gods won't believe me when I tell them this story. You've heard the proverb about the elephant that passed through the eye of the needle, but his tail got stuck? And now King Yudhishtra, after having gained the merit that even gods dream about gaining, gets stuck by a dog's tail. Ha! Ha!" Lord Indra got back in his space chariot, which lifted off the ground.

"Come," Yudhishtra said, turning to the dog. "I will roam this void rather than abandon you."

When Yudhishtra turned around, he saw that the dog had vanished and in his stead stood Lord Dharma, glowing with health and vitality, his arms wide open, his breastplate casting a circle of warm, bright light.

"My son!" said Lord Dharma, embracing Yudhishtra. "How very proud I am of you, who love, respect, and protect the speechless creatures of the earth. I expected nothing less from you. Ah, Yudhishtra, you above all else deserve to go to heaven for your insight, and for your connection to the entire created world. Come!"

"I look forward to a long rest," Yudhishtra said, climbing onto the chariot with Dharma by his side.

"Rest?" laughed Indra. "Just a brief, but adequate one. Every end is a beginning, king. Many worlds await you. Come!"

ACKNOWLEDGMENTS

I wish to thank Raoul Goff, president of Mandala Publishing, for giving me the opportunity to write this book; Kelly Thompson for bringing Raoul to our home and introducing us; my editors, Mariah Bear for her stimulating ideas, and Diana Reiss for being patient and gentle in the editorial process; Charles Levine (Fonfer Jee) who has helped and encouraged me in so many areas; Ramgopal Bajaj, who told me the two stories, "The Bird Who Fought War," and "Blind Hunger," told to him by the best of poets, S.H. Vatsyayan (Ageye); the staff of Behta Pani, Himmat Ram, Mira, Raju and Amar; Charanjit Singh of Core PR, and Avnish Katoch for website support; the late Donald Dean Powell, whose brief poem appears in "The Marriage of Shiva and Parvati"; David and Jessica Wallack, for their support and enthusiasm; Payson R. Stevens for helping to shape many of these stories with his constant feedback, his creative ideas, and his love and enthusiastic support.

"On the Track of Love" was adapted and retold from a brief mention of the story in Isaac A. Ezekiel's *Kabir, The Great Mystic* (Punjab: Radha Soami Satsang Beas, 1973).

"Entirely Entangled" was adapted and retold from Heinrich Zimmer's *Myths and Symbols in Indian Art and Civilization* (New York: Pantheon Books, 1953). This is a well-known myth, and I was familiar with it before I encountered it again in Zimmer.

"Vishnu Forgets" was garnered from various sources, now forgotten.

"Out of the Mouth" was adapted and retold from Heinrich Zimmer's *Myths and Symbols in Indian Art and Civilization* (New York: Pantheon Books, 1953).

"How Brahma Birthed the World" was adapted and retold from Eknath Easwaran's *Thousand Names of Vishnu* (New Delhi: Jaico Books, 2003).

"Indra Gets Caught" was adapted from William S. Buck's adaptation of *The Ramayana* (Berkeley and Los Angeles: University of California Press, 1976)

"The Marriage of Shiva and Parvati" was adapted and retold from various sources, now forgotten.

"The Birth of Ganesha" was adapted and retold from John Dowson's *A Classical Dictionary of Hindu Mythology and Religion* (New Delhi: Rupa and Co, 2005), and Royina Grewal's *The Book of Ganesh* (New Delhi: Penguin Books, 2001)

"Ganesha Goes to Lunch" was adapted and retold from *Tales of Ganesh* (New Delhi: Nitu Mehta Publications, 2005), and Royina Grewal's *The Book of Ganesh* (New Delhi, Penguin Books, 2001)

"The Million Steps" was told to me by Ramgopal Bajaj, and my father, Hardit Singh Kapur, from a story written by Bhai Gurdas.

"The Snake Who Lost His Hiss" was adapted from a tale by Sri Ramakrishna.

"Hermits," and "From the Eyes of Stars" were developed from brief references in Isaac Ezekiel's *Kabir, The Great Mystic* (Punjab: Radha Soami Satsang Beas, 1973).

"The Sinews of His Spirit" was adapted and retold from William S. Buck's adaptation of *The Ramayana* (Berkeley and Los Angeles: University of California Press, 1976).

"Ashes and Dust" was adapted and retold from C. Rajagopalachari's translation of *The Ramayana* (Mumbai: Bharaitya Vidya Bhawan, 2005).

"The Toad Who Didn't Croak" was adapted and retold from a brief mention of the story in Isaac Ezekiel's *Kabir, The Great Mystic* (Punjab: Radha Soami Satsang Beas, 1973).

"Hanuman Bares All" was adapted from William S. Buck's adaptation of *The Ramayana* (Berkeley and Los Angeles: University of California Press, 1976)

"The Holy, Lowly Staff" was adapted from Ramesh Menon's translation of *The Ramayana* (New Delhi: HarperCollins Publishers, 2003)

"The Deer People" was adapted from William S. Buck's adaptation of *Mahabharata* (Berkeley, Los Angeles, and London: University of California Press, 1973).

"See Him in the Dark" was adapted from William S. Buck's adaptation of *Mahabharata* (Berkeley, Los Angeles, and London: University of California Press, 1973), and Ananda K. Coomaraswamy and Sister Nivedita's *Myths of the Hindus and Buddhists* (New York: Dover, 1967).

"You" was adapted from William S. Buck's adaptation of *Mahabharata* (Berkeley, Los Angeles, and London: University of California Press, 1973), and Ananda K. Coomaraswamy and Sister Nivedita's *Myths of the Hindus and Buddhists* (New York: Dover, 1967).

"The Bird Who Fought War," and "Blind Hunger" were told to me by Ramgopal Bajaj, who heard them from S. H. Vatsyayan, the preeminent Hindi poet of the twentieth century. I have not found them anywhere in my research.

"Elsewhere Bound" was adapted and retold from William S. Buck's adaptation of *Mahabharata* (Berkeley, Los Angeles, and London: University of California Press, 1973), and Ananda K. Coomaraswamy and Sister Nivedita's *Myths of the Hindus and Buddhists* (New York: Dover, 1967).